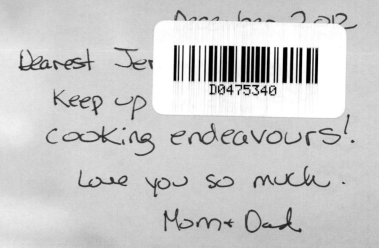

Dearest Jer
Keep up
cooking endeavours!
Love you so much.
Mom+Dad

December 2012

Grandma's Recipes

igloo

Published in 2012
by Igloo Books Ltd
Cottage Farm
Sywell
Northants
NN6 0BJ
www.igloo-books.com

Copyright © 2011 Igloo Books Ltd

All rights reserved. No part of this publication may be reproduced,
stored in a retrieval system, or transmitted in any way or by any means,electronic,
mechanical, photocopying, recording or otherwise, without the prior written
permission of the publisher.

B044 0212
2 4 6 8 10 9 7 5 3

ISBN: 978-0-85734-761-9

Printed and manufactured in China

Contents

Introduction

This book is packed full of wonderful ideas to celebrate those classic recipes that have been passed down from generation to generation in Grandma's kitchen. Everyone remembers dishes cooked by our parents and grandparents that we enjoyed in childhood, and that brought us comfort.

As we all come from different walks of life, capturing the essence of what Grandma's recipes means to different people can be hard, but everyone instinctively knows what it means. Often, we think of simple recipes full of satisfying flavour, which are not only mouth-wateringly delicious, but create nostalgic memories of childhood, family warmth and Grandma's indulgence.

The recipes that follow are split into five instantly recognisable chapters to help you recreate these classics. Who can resist Grandma's sweet treats? There are a selection of cookies, brownies, tarts and cakes to get your taste buds tingling, from old fashioned jam tarts, to indulgent peanut caramel squares.

Then there are savoury snacks, who could forget irresistible cheese straws, beautiful quiches and homemade savoury tarts that Grandma always seemed to have readymade, still warm from the oven.

For something a little more substantial, the homemade meals section is bursting with scrumptious traditional dishes and some exciting new ideas. For those who always loved Grandma's Lancashire hotpot, but didn't know how to make it, the recipe in this book is simple, easy-to-follow and tastes great!

Sometimes only a good old fashioned dessert will hit the spot! There are plenty to choose from, like lemon meringue pie, sticky toffee pudding and a classic pavlova. Let's face it; a delicious dessert is the perfect ending to every meal.

And finally, who can forget walking in to Grandma's kitchen and smelling the aroma of freshly baked bread? So we've dedicated a whole chapter to breads, such as traditional banana loaves and soda bread to new and exciting ideas – why not try yummy chocolate plaits or gooey cinnamon rolls?

The most important thing about these recipes is the pleasure and enjoyment we get from cooking and eating them. After all, nothing can compare to the nostalgia of baking classic recipes passed down through the generations. But these recipes are just the start, hopefully you will find the inspiration to create recipes and memories that you can pass down through your own family.

Sweet treats

Raspberry and orange tartlets

MAKES

16 tartlets

PREP AND COOK TIME

55 minutes

INGREDIENTS

200 g | 7 oz | 1 ¾ cups plain
(all-purpose) flour

50 g | 2 oz | ¼ cup caster (superfine) sugar

a pinch of salt

100 g | 3 ½ oz | ½ cup butter

1 egg

1 tbsp water

For the jam:

1 large orange

250 g | 9 oz | 2 cups raspberries

250 g | 9 oz | 1 ¼ cups jam sugar

1 lemon, juice

1 tbsp orange liqueur

For the jam, peel and segment the orange, reserving the juice and cut the segments into pieces.

Mix the orange segments, juice and raspberries with the sugar and lemon juice in a pan and increase the heat to boiling point. Boil vigorously for about 3 minutes, skimming off the top of the contents. Transfer the mixture to a bowl, stir in the liqueur and leave it to cool.

For the pastry, mix the flour with the sugar and salt in a mixing bowl. Rub in the butter until the mixture resembles breadcrumbs. Stir in the egg and water and combine to form a dough. Wrap and chill the dough for 30 minutes.

Heat the oven to 200°C (180° fan) 400F, gas 6. Butter a shallow tart tin with 16 holes, each 5 cm / 2 " in diameter.

Roll out the pastry on a lightly floured surface. Cut out 16 circles and line the tart tins. Prick the bases with a fork. Bake the pastry cases for 12-15 minutes, until lightly browned then place on a wire rack to cool.

Spoon the cooled jam into the tart cases.

Brownies

MAKES

16 brownies

PREP AND COOK TIME

55 minutes

INGREDIENTS

200 g | 7 oz plain chocolate

200 g | 7 oz white chocolate

250 g | 9 oz | 1 cup unsalted butter

300 g | 11 oz | 1 ½ cups caster (superfine) sugar

4 eggs, beaten

140 g | 5 oz | 1 ½ cups plain
(all-purpose) flour

Heat the oven to 180°C (160° fan) 350F, gas 4. Grease a 23 cm / 9 " square tin with butter.

Put the plain and white chocolate into two separate bowls and add half of the butter to each. Melt over a pan of simmering water. Stir until the chocolate and butter are blended.

Add half the sugar and 2 beaten eggs to each bowl, then beat until smooth. Stir 50 g of the flour into the plain chocolate mixture and the remaining flour into the white mixture.

Spoon tablespoons of the mixture into the tin, alternating plain and white chocolate to make a patchwork pattern. When the base of the tin is covered, spoon more mixture over the first layer, placing the white chocolate mixture over the plain chocolate mixture, and vice versa. Drag a skewer through the tin several times to create a marbled effect.

Bake for 35 minutes, until the middle is set. Leave to cool in the tin before cutting it into squares.

Walnut caramel slices

MAKES

12 slices

PREP AND COOK TIME

1 hour

INGREDIENTS

350 g | 12 oz | 1 ½ cups butter

225 g | 8 oz | 1 cup sugar

275 g | 10 oz | 2 ⅔ cups plain
(all-purpose) flour

400 ml | 14 fl. oz | 1 ¾ cups condensed milk

60 ml | 2 fl. oz | ¼ cup honey

3 tbsp walnuts, roughly chopped

230 g | 8 oz dark (plain) chocolate

For the biscuit base, heat the oven to 180°C (160° fan) 350F, gas 4 and grease a 20 cm square baking tin with butter.

Beat 225 g of the butter with 100 g of the sugar until smooth. Sift in the flour and mix to a soft, biscuit dough.

Press the dough smoothly into the tin and bake for 25-30 minutes until golden.

For the topping, melt the remaining butter in a pan, add the remaining sugar, the condensed milk and the honey. Increase the heat to boiling point and simmer, stirring constantly, for about 5 minutes, until the mixture becomes brown and thickened.

Stir in the walnuts, then pour over the base and leave to cool.

Melt the chocolate in a heatproof bowl over a pan of simmering water. Pour over the caramel and leave to cool for at least 3 hours.

Chocolate cake

SERVES

6-8 people

PREP AND COOK TIME

1 hour 25 minutes

INGREDIENTS

200 g | 7 oz plain dark (plain)
chocolate, chopped

200 g | 7 oz | 1 cup butter

150 g | 5 oz | 1 ½ cups icing
(confectioners') sugar

8 eggs, separated

100 g | 3 ½ oz | ½ cup sugar

150 g | 5 oz | 1 ¼ cups plain (all-purpose) flour

50 g | 2 oz | ½ cup ground almonds

150 g | 5 oz plain dark (plain)
chocolate, chopped

Preheat the oven to 190°C (170° fan) 375F, gas 5 and grease a loaf tin with butter.

Melt 150 g of the chocolate in a heatproof bowl over a pan of simmering water.

Beat the butter and icing sugar in a mixing bowl until light and fluffy. Gradually add the egg yolks and melted chocolate to the butter and stir until blended.

Whisk the egg whites and sugar until stiff and fold carefully into the chocolate mixture.

Chop the remaining chocolate and mix with the flour and almonds and fold into the mixture.

Pour into the loaf tin and bake for an hour until cooked through. Cool the cake in the tin for 10 minutes, then place on a wire rack to cool completely.

For the topping, melt the chocolate over simmering water and leave to cool and thicken. Pour the chocolate over the cake and leave it to set.

Madeleines

MAKES

24 madeleines

PREP AND COOK TIME

25 minutes

INGREDIENTS

125 g | 4 ½ oz | ½ cup sugar

100 g | 3 ½ oz | ½ cup butter

125 g | 4 ½ oz | 1 cup plain (all-purpose) flour

a pinch of salt

3 eggs

1 tsp rosewater

icing (confectioners') sugar, to decorate

Beat the butter and sugar in a mixing bowl until creamy, then beat in the eggs until blended. Stir in the flour, salt and rosewater. Cover the bowl and leave it to chill in the fridge for an hour.

Heat the oven to 180°C (160° fan) 350F, gas 4. Grease a 24 hole madeleine tin with butter.

Spoon the mixture into the moulds and bake for 15 minutes, until golden. Remove the tin from the oven and allow the madeleines to cool for a few minutes. Place the them on a wire rack to cool completely.

Sift a little icing sugar over them before serving.

Muesli fingers

MAKES

12 fingers

PREP AND COOK TIME

30 minutes

INGREDIENTS

110 g | 4 oz | ½ cup butter

85 g | 3 oz | ⅓ cup light brown sugar

75 g | 2 ½ oz | ½ cup golden (corn) syrup

275 g | 10 oz | 4 cups high fruit muesli

1 tbsp pumpkin seeds

Preheat the oven to 180°C (160° fan) 350F, gas 4 and line a baking tin with greaseproof paper.

Heat the butter, sugar and golden syrup in a saucepan over a medium heat until just melted.

Add the muesli and pumpkin seeds and mix well, then tip the mixture into the baking tin and spread evenly.

Bake for 15-20 minutes until golden. Mark it into 12 bars and leave to cool completely in the tin, as it falls apart when warm, and then cut when cold.

Peanut biscuits

MAKES

16 biscuits

PREP AND COOK TIME

55 minutes

INGREDIENTS

110 g | 4 oz | ½ cup butter

450 g | 16 oz | 4 cups plain (all-purpose) flour

4 tbsp caster (superfine) sugar

85 g | 3 oz crunchy peanut butter

2 egg yolks

Heat the oven to 180°C (160° fan) 350F, gas 4 and line a baking tray with greaseproof paper.

Mix the flour, sugar, peanut butter, egg yolks and butter together in a mixing bowl to form a smooth dough.

Break off evenly sized pieces of the dough and roll into walnut-sized balls.

Place the dough balls onto the baking tray and gently press each ball with the back of a fork to flatten slightly.

Bake for 10 minutes until just golden. Cool the biscuits on the tray for 5 minutes, then place them on a wire rack to cool completely.

Marbled
chocolate meringue

MAKES

20 meringues

PREP AND COOK TIME

55 minutes

INGREDIENTS

5 egg whites

200 g | 7 oz | 2 cups icing (confectioners') sugar

a pinch of salt

100 g | 3 ½ oz plain chocolate, melted

Heat the oven to 140°C (120°C fan) 275F, gas 1. Line a baking tray with greaseproof paper.

Whisk the egg whites with the icing sugar and salt until stiff. Drizzle the melted chocolate over the egg whites and fold in with a spatula until the mixture is slightly marbled.

Using a tablespoon, spoon the meringue mixture onto the baking tray. Bake for 35-45 minutes until the meringues are crisp on the outside, but soft inside. Turn the oven off, and leave the meringues to cool.

Lemon squares

MAKES

12-15 squares

PREP AND COOK TIME

1 hour 10 minutes

INGREDIENTS

250 g | 9 oz | 1 cup butter

125 g | 4 ½ oz | ½ cup sugar

250 g | 9 oz | 2 ½ cups plain (all-purpose) flour

a pinch of salt

For the topping:

2 eggs

250 g | 9 oz | 1 ½ cups sugar

2 tbsp flour

a pinch of salt

2 lemons, juice and zest

icing (confectioners') sugar, to decorate

Heat the oven to 160°C (140° fan) 325F, gas 3. Grease a rectangular or square baking tin with butter.

Beat the butter with the sugar in a mixing bowl until creamy. Add the flour and salt and mix to a smooth dough. Press the dough into the base of the baking tin. Bake for 20 minutes until cooked and golden.

Beat the eggs with the sugar until foamy. Mix in the flour, salt, lemon juice and zest. Pour the mixture over the cooled base. Bake for a further 25-30 minutes until the filling is set. Remove from the oven and leave it in the tin to cool.

Slice into small squares and sift over the icing sugar.

Fruit cake

MAKES
1 cake

PREP AND COOK TIME
2 hours 20 minutes

INGREDIENTS
225 g | 8 oz | 1 cup butter

225 g | 8 oz | 1 cup caster (superfine) sugar

5 eggs

225 g | 8 oz | 2 cups self-raising flour

½ tsp grated nutmeg

75 g | 2 ½ oz | ½ cup glace (candied) cherries, rinsed, dried and quartered

175 g | 6 oz | 1 cup currants

175 g | 6 oz | 1 cup sultanas

50 g | 2 oz | 1 cup candied peel, diced

4 tbsp milk

75 g | 2 ½ oz | ½ cup ground almonds

Heat the oven to 170°C (150° fan) 300F, gas 3. Grease and line a 22 cm / 9 " square cake tin with greaseproof baking paper.

Beat the butter and sugar together in a mixing bowl until light and fluffy. Add the eggs, one at a time along with a teaspoon of flour, beating well after each addition.

Sift the remaining flour with the nutmeg and fold into the mixture. Fold in the fruits and candied peel and mix well.

Gently fold in the milk and ground almonds. Spoon into the tin and use the back of the spoon to slightly hollow the centre.

Bake for 1½-2 hours until cooked through. Test with a wooden toothpick, if it comes out clean, the cake is cooked. Cool in the tin for 10 minutes, then place on a wire rack to cool further.

Chocolate chip cookies

MAKES

24 cookies

PREP AND COOK TIME

55 minutes

INGREDIENTS

225 g | 8 oz | 1 cup butter

175 g | 6 oz | ¾ cup caster
(superfine) sugar

175 g | 6 oz | 1 cup light brown sugar

1 tsp vanilla extract

350 g | 12 oz | 3 cups plain
(all-purpose) flour

1 tsp bicarbonate of soda (baking soda)

350 g | 12 oz | 2 cups chocolate chips

2 eggs

1 tsp salt

Heat the oven to 190°C (170° fan) 375F, gas 5 and lightly grease 2 large baking trays with oil.

Beat the butter, sugar, brown sugar and vanilla in a mixing bowl until creamy. Beat in the eggs until smooth.

Sift in the flour, bicarbonate of soda and salt and stir well. Stir in the chocolate chips.

Divide the dough into 2 equal portions. Roll each into a log shape 5 cm / 2 " in diameter, wrap them in cling film and chill for at least 30 minutes.

Cut the logs into slices 2 cm / ¾ " thick and place on the baking trays, widely spaced apart. Bake for 9-12 minutes until golden brown. Cool the cookies on the trays for 5 minutes, then place on a wire rack to cool completely.

Shortbread

MAKES

1 cake

PREP AND COOK TIME

1 hour 10 minutes

INGREDIENTS

225 g | 8 oz | 2 cups plain
(all-purpose) flour

110 g | 4 oz | 1 cup cornflour (cornstarch)

110 g | 4 oz | 1 cup icing (confectioners') sugar

225 g | 8 oz | 1 cup unsalted butter

caster (superfine) sugar, to decorate

Heat the oven to 150°C (130° fan) 300F, gas 2. Grease a round cake tin with butter.

Sift the flour, cornflour and icing sugar into a mixing bowl. Knead in the butter and mix to a soft dough.

Pat the dough out into a round cake tin, 2 ½ cm / 1 " thick to fit the cake tin. Prick the top with a fork.

Bake for 50 minutes, until cooked. Remove from the oven and sprinkle with caster sugar and place it back in the oven to bake for a further 10 minutes. Carefully remove and place on a wire rack to cool.

Date cake

MAKES

1 loaf

PREP AND COOK TIME

1 hour 15 minutes

INGREDIENTS

170 ml | 6 fl. oz | ¾ cup boiling water

1 tsp bicarbonate of soda (baking soda)

175 g | 6 oz | 1 cup chopped pitted dates

125 g | 4 ½ oz | ½ cup butter

125 g | 4 ½ oz | ½ cup light brown sugar

1 egg, beaten

250 g | 9 oz | 2 ¼ cups plain (all-purpose) flour

4 tbsp sugar crystals

Heat the oven to 170°C (150° fan) 300F, gas 3 and grease a loaf tin with butter.

Mix a tablespoonful of boiling water with the bicarbonate of soda and pour over the dates.

Beat the butter and sugar in a mixing bowl until light and fluffy. Gradually beat in the egg until smooth.

Stir in the flour and sugar crystals, add the dates and the liquid and stir together well.

Spoon the mixture into the loaf tin and bake for about an hour. Insert a wooden toothpick into the centre of the cake, if it comes out clean, the cake is done. Allow the cake to cool in the tin, then it turn out onto a wire rack to cool completely.

Peanut cookies

MAKES

25-30 cookies

PREP AND COOK TIME

25 minutes

INGREDIENTS

120 g | 4 oz | ½ cup butter

150 g | 5 oz | 1 cup brown sugar

1 egg, beaten

150 g | 5 oz | 1 ½ cups plain
(all-purpose) flour

1 tsp baking powder

½ tsp ground cinnamon

½ tsp grated nutmeg

1 orange, grated zest

40 g | 1 ½ oz | ½ cup whole, unsalted peanuts

100 g | 3 ½ oz | 1 cup unsalted peanuts,
roughly chopped

80 g | 3 oz | 1 cup oats

Heat the oven to 200°C (180° fan) 400F, gas 6. Line a large baking tray with greaseproof baking paper.

Beat the butter and sugar in a mixing bowl until creamy and then stir in the egg.

Mix the flour, baking powder, cinnamon, nutmeg and orange zest together and stir into the butter mixture. Stir in the whole peanuts, 60 g of the chopped peanuts and the oats.

Shape the mixture into round balls. Place the balls on the baking tray, wide apart and sprinkle with the remaining chopped peanuts.

Bake for 15 minutes until golden. Allow to cool on the baking tray for 5 minutes then place on a wire rack to cool completely.

Apple muffins

MAKES

12 muffins

PREP AND COOK TIME

35 minutes

INGREDIENTS

30 g | 1 oz butter

30 g | 1 oz demerara sugar

30 g | 1 oz ground almonds

60 g | 2 oz sunflower seeds

225 g | 8 oz | 2 cups plain (all-purpose) flour

2 tsp baking powder

75 g | 2 ½ oz | ½ cup brown sugar

1 tsp mixed spice

2 apples, cored and cubed

1 egg

150 ml | 5 fl. oz | 1 cup soured cream

50 g | 2 oz | ½ cup butter, melted

Rub the butter into the flour, sugar and almonds until the mixture resembles breadcrumbs. Stir in the sunflower seeds and set aside as this will be used as a topping.

Heat the oven to 190°C (170° fan) 375F, gas 5. Line a 12 hole muffin tin with paper cases.

Sift the flour and baking powder into a mixing bowl. Stir in the sugar, mixed spice and apple.

Mix together the egg, soured cream and melted butter. Mix the wet and dry ingredients together, and stir lightly. The mixture will be lumpy.

Spoon the mixture into the paper cases, sprinkle over the topping and bake for 15-20 minutes until the muffins are well risen and firm.

Place on a wire rack to cool.

Cinnamon biscuits

MAKES

20 biscuits

PREP AND COOK TIME

1 hour

INGREDIENTS

250 g | 9 oz | 2 ¼ cups plain (all-purpose) flour

1 tbsp ground cinnamon

½ tsp salt

125 g | 4 ½ oz | ½ cup unsalted butter

110 g | 4 oz | ½ cup caster (superfine) sugar

1 tsp vanilla extract

1 egg, beaten

Heat the oven to 180°C (160° fan) 350F, gas 4 and line a large baking tray with greaseproof paper.

Sift the flour, cinnamon and salt into a mixing bowl. Rub in the butter until the mixture resembles breadcrumbs.

Stir in the sugar and vanilla. Beat in the egg and mix it to a smooth dough. Wrap the dough in cling film and chill for 30 minutes.

Roll out the dough thinly on a lightly floured surface and cut into rounds with a cookie cutter.

Place the rounds on the lined baking tray and bake for 12-15 minutes until lightly golden. Cool on the tray for a few minutes, then place on a wire rack to cool completely.

Chocolate traybake

MAKES

24 squares

PREP AND COOK TIME

1 hour 15 minutes

INGREDIENTS

200 g | 7 oz | 1 cup butter

150 g | 5 oz | 1 ½ cups icing (confectioners') sugar

8 eggs, separated

150 g | 5 oz plain dark (plain) chocolate, melted

100 g | 3 ½ oz | ½ cup sugar

150 g | 5 oz | 1 ⅓ cups plain (all -purpose) flour

50 g | 2 oz | ⅓ cup unsalted peanuts, crushed

60 g | 2 oz cocoa powder

Heat the oven to 180°C (160° fan) 350F, gas 4. Line a 20 cm x 30 cm / 8 " x 12 " baking tin with greaseproof paper.

Beat the butter with the icing sugar in a mixing bowl until light and fluffy. Gradually beat in the egg yolks and melted chocolate until it is smooth.

Whisk the egg whites with the sugar until they form stiff peaks, then carefully fold into the chocolate mixture.

Mix the flour with the crushed peanuts and cocoa and fold in. Spread the mixture into the tin and bake for 35-40 minutes. Test by inserting a wooden toothpick, if it comes out clean, the cake is done. Allow it to cool in the tin.

For the topping, heat the cream in a pan with the chocolate, over a low heat and stir until melted. Cool slightly then spread on top of the cake and sprinkle with peanuts. Cut the cake into pieces when the icing has set.

Sultana Scones

MAKES

12 scones

PREP AND COOK TIME

30 minutes

INGREDIENTS

225 g | 8 oz | 2 cups plain (all -purpose) flour

½ tsp bicarbonate of soda (baking soda)

½ tsp cream of tartar

50 g | 2 oz | ¼ cup butter

50 g | 2 oz | ¼ cup caster sugar

50 g | 2 oz | ⅓ cup sultanas

150 ml | 5 fl. oz | ⅔ cup milk

Heat the oven to 220°C (200° fan) 425F, gas 7 and grease and flour a baking tray.

Sift the flour, bicarbonate of soda and cream of tartar into a large mixing bowl. Lightly rub in the butter until the mixture resembles breadcrumbs.

Stir in the sugar and sultanas. Make a well in the centre and pour in the milk and mix to form a soft dough, then turn it out on to a lightly floured surface.

Lightly knead the dough until smooth and then roll or pat it out to a 1 cm / ½ " thickness. Cut out rounds using a 5 cm / 2 " cookie cutter.

Place the scones on the baking tray and bake for 10-15 minutes, until risen and golden. Place them on a wire rack to cool completely. Serve with clotted cream and strawberry jam.

Florentines

MAKES

12 florentines

PREP AND COOK TIME

25 minutes

INGREDIENTS

25 g | 1 oz butter

75 g | 2 ½ oz | ½ cup caster (superfine) sugar

2 tsp plain (all-purpose) flour

45 ml | 1 ½ fl. oz cream

110 g | 4 oz | ½ cup chopped fruit

50 g | 2 oz | 1 cup flaked almonds

75 g | 2 ½ oz plain chocolate

Heat the oven to 180°C (160° fan) 350F, gas 4. Line a 12 hole bun tin with greaseproof paper.

Heat the butter and sugar in a pan until melted and golden brown. Remove from the heat and stir in the flour and cream. Add the fruit and nuts and mix together well.

Spoon into the tins and spread out with a teaspoon. Bake for 12-15 minutes until golden brown. Cool in the tins for 10-15 minutes then remove and peel off the baking paper.

Melt the chocolate in a heatproof bowl over a pan of simmering water. Spread a little chocolate onto the flat side of each florentine and allow it to set.

Peanut caramel squares

MAKES

40 squares

PREP AND COOK TIME

1 hour 50 minutes

INGREDIENTS

300 g | 11 oz | 1 ⅓ cups butter

150 g | 5 oz | ¾ cup sugar

1 egg

2 egg yolks

400 g | 14 oz | 3 ½ cups plain (all-purpose) flour

1 tsp ground cinnamon

50 g | 2 oz | ½ cup cocoa powder

50 g | 2 oz | ½ cup grated dark (plain) chocolate

For the caramel:

300 g | 11 oz | 1 ½ cups sugar

75 ml | 2 ½ fl. oz water

250 g | 9 oz | 2 ¼ cups

chopped peanuts

200 ml | 7 fl. oz | ⅞ cup cream

a pinch of salt

1 tbsp butter

For the base, beat the butter and sugar in a mixing bowl until fluffy. Beat in the egg and egg yolks.

Mix the flour, cinnamon, cocoa powder and grated chocolate together and stir half of the flour mixture into the butter mixture. Add the remaining flour mixture and mix with your hands to form a dough. Wrap the dough in cling film and chill for an hour.

Heat the oven to 180°C (160° fan) 350F, gas 4. Line a 30 cm x 40 cm / 12 " x 16 " baking tin with greaseproof paper.

Line the baking tin with the dough and bake for 20-25 minutes until golden.

For the caramel, heat the sugar and water in a pan until the sugar has dissolved. Increase the heat to boiling point and stir in the peanuts. Add the cream and salt and cook on a high heat until the mixture is dark golden brown, then stir in the butter.

Pour the caramel mixture over the cooked base and leave it to set. Cut into small pieces with a sharp knife before it hardens completely.

Cherry and coconut slices

MAKES

24 slices

PREP AND COOK TIME

1 hour 45 minutes

INGREDIENTS

200 g | 7 oz | 3 cups desiccated (flaked) coconut

400 g | 14 oz | 2 cups sugar

400 g | 14 oz | 2 cups butter

8 eggs

400 g | 14 oz | 3 ¾ cups plain (all-purpose) flour

3 tsp baking powder

20 ml | ¾ fl. oz coconut syrup

2 tsp cherry liqueur

2 tbsp milk, if needed

To decorate:

300 g | 11 oz milk chocolate

75 g | 2 ½ oz | ⅓ cup butter

100 g | 3 ½ oz | ½ cup glace (candied) cherries

For the base, heat the oven to 180°C (160° fan) 350F, gas 4 and line a rectangular baking tin with greaseproof paper.

Toast the coconut until golden in a dry frying pan. Sprinkle the pan with 4-6 tablespoons of sugar and stir over the heat until the coconut is lightly caramelised. Set aside and leave it to cool.

Cream the butter and sugar in a mixing bowl until light and fluffy. Beat in the eggs until smooth.

Roughly grind the caramelised coconut in a food processor or pestle and mortar.

Sift the flour and baking powder in to the egg mixture. Stir in the coconut. Gradually add the coconut syrup and liqueur. If the mixture is too stiff, add a tablespoonful of milk at a time.

Spread the mixture in the baking tin and bake for 60 minutes until firm.

Place the cake on a wire rack and remove the paper, then leave it to cool.

For the icing, put the chocolate and butter into a heatproof bowl and melt over a pan of simmering water.

Spread the icing over the cake and scatter with the candied fruit. When the chocolate is almost set, cut the cake into 24 pieces and leave it to cool completely.

Savoury snacks

Egg and bacon muffins

SERVES

4

PREP AND COOK TIME

15 minutes

INGREDIENTS

4 eggs

2 English muffins

12 slices streaky bacon

Heat the grill to its highest setting. Heat a pan of water to boiling point and carefully put in the eggs. Boil for 3 minutes and remove from the pan.

Put the bacon under the grill and cook on both sides until crisp. Slice the muffins in half and toast them under the grill for a few minutes. Place 3 slices of bacon on each muffin half.

Peel the egg shells and place the eggs on top of the bacon. Serve immediately.

Pumpkin soup

SERVES

4

PREP AND COOK TIME

45 minutes

INGREDIENTS

2 tbsp butter

1 onion, finely chopped

1 garlic clove, finely chopped

150 g | 5 oz | ¾ cup diced floury potatoes

500 g | 1 lb | 2 cups diced pumpkin flesh

650 ml | 23 fl. oz | 2 ⅔ cups vegetable stock

100 ml | 3 ½ fl. oz cream

10 g | ¼ oz fresh ginger, grated

½ tsp lemon juice

salt and ground black pepper

a pinch of grated nutmeg

100 g | 3 ½ oz | ½ cup diced bacon

25 g | 1 oz butter

5 fresh sage leaves

Heat the butter in a pan and fry the onion and garlic over a medium heat until soft and translucent. Add the potatoes and pumpkin and cook for a few minutes.

Stir in the vegetable stock and cook for 25 minutes until the vegetables are soft. Purée in a blender or push through a sieve and add the cream. Add a little more stock if desired.

Add the ginger and season with lemon juice, salt, pepper and nutmeg.

Fry the bacon in a small pan in the butter until crisp. Remove from the pan and drain on kitchen paper. Add the sage to the pan and fry for 30 seconds.

Add the bacon and sage to the soup, drizzle with the olive oil and season with ground black pepper.

Cheese straws

MAKES

12 straws

PREP AND COOK TIME

25 minutes

INGREDIENTS

400 g | 14 oz puff pastry

1 egg yolk

2 tbsp water

90 g | 3 oz grated Parmesan cheese

1 tsp paprika

Heat the oven to 220°C (200° fan) 425F, gas 7. Line a baking tray with greaseproof paper.

Roll the pastry out into a large square. Whisk the egg yolk with the water and brush half over the pastry.

Sprinkle grated cheese and paprika over the pastry. Fold once to cover the filling, then flatten slightly. Brush the top with the remaining egg yolk.

Cut the pastry into thin strips about 1 ½ cm / ½ " wide. Twist the pastry strips to form spirals and place on the baking tray.

Bake for about 12 minutes until golden brown.

Asparagus tart

SERVES

4

PREP AND COOK TIME

55 minutes

INGREDIENTS

375 g | 13 oz shortcrust
pastry, readymade
450 g | 1 lb asparagus, ends trimmed
2 eggs, plus 1 egg yolk
225 ml | 8 fl. oz | 1 cup cream
150 g | 5 oz | 1 ½ cups grated Parmesan

Heat the oven to 190°C (170° fan) 375F, gas 5. Grease a rectangular tart tin, roughly 33 cm x 10 cm / 13 " x 4 " with butter.

Roll out the pastry and line the tart tin. Place greaseproof paper on the base and fill with baking beans and bake for 10 minutes. Remove the paper and baking beans and bake for a further 5 minutes.

Blanch the asparagus in boiling, salted water for 2 minutes then drain and cool. Arrange the asparagus over the base of the pastry.

Beat the eggs, egg yolk, cream and chives together and season well with salt and pepper. Pour the mixture over the asparagus and sprinkle with the cheese.

Bake for 20 minutes until set and lightly golden. Allow the tart to stand for 15 minutes before serving.

Ham and egg pie

SERVES

8

PREP AND COOK TIME

2 hours

INGREDIENTS

6 eggs

400 g | 14 oz | 2 cups minced (ground) pork

200 g | 7 oz pork sausage meat

140 g | 5 oz | 1 cup cooked ham, chopped

1 small onion, finely chopped

salt and pepper

For the pastry:

450 g | 1 lb | 4 cups plain (all-purpose) flour

2 tsp salt

100 g | 3 ½ oz | ½ cup lard

60 ml | 2 fl. oz milk

150 ml | 5 fl. oz | ⅔ cup water

1 egg, beaten

Grease a 1 litre terrine or tin with butter.

For the filling, boil a large saucepan of water with the eggs in for 7-8 minutes. Cool in cold water, peel off the shells and set aside. Mix the pork, sausage meat, ham and onion together in a large bowl. Season generously and mix well until combined.

For the pastry, put the flour into a mixing bowl with the salt. Heat the lard, milk and water in a saucepan until the lard has completely melted. Pour the milk mixture into the flour and beat until combined. Turn the mixture out onto a floured surface and knead to form a dough. Heat the oven to 200°C (180° fan) 400F, gas 6.

Roll out ⅔ of the dough into a rectangle roughly the width and length of the baking dish. Lay the dough in the terrine and press it into the base and up the sides of the dish until it comes to the top and hangs over the rim. Spoon half the meat mixture into the terrine dish and press it down. Make a channel down the middle of the meat. Trim the tops and bottoms off the eggs and lay them in a row, along the channel.

Spoon the remaining meat mixture over the eggs, and press it down, so it is compacted. Brush the overhang of the pastry with the beaten egg, then roll out the rest of the pastry to fit over the pie.Pinch the edges together to seal. Brush the top with the beaten egg and pierce three holes along the top the bake for 30 minutes. Reduce the oven temperature to 180°C (160° fan) 350F, gas 4 and bake for a further hour. Leave to cool in the terrine.

Welsh rarebit

SERVES

4

PREP AND COOK TIME

20 minutes

INGREDIENTS

125 ml | 4 ½ fl. oz | ½ cup milk

1 tbsp flour

400 g | 14 oz | 4 cups Cheddar cheese, grated

175 g | 6 oz | 3 ½ cups breadcrumbs

1 tsp English mustard powder

2 tbsp Worcestershire sauce

120 ml | 4 fl. oz | ½ cup dark ale

5-9 eggs

pepper

6-8 slices, toasted crusty bread

fresh parsley, chopped

For the rarebit, heat the milk in a pan, whisk in the flour and increase the heat to boiling point. Cook for about 1 minute until slightly thickened.

Reduce the heat and add the grated cheese. Stir briefly until melted, then add the breadcrumbs, mustard powder, Worcestershire sauce and ale. Stir the mixture until it starts to leave the sides of the pan. Remove from the heat and leave to cool slightly.

Beat in an egg and season with pepper.

Heat the grill. Spread the cheese mixture onto the toast and grill until browned and golden.

To poach the eggs, put cold water into a deep pan. Increase the heat to boiling point, then reduce the heat a little to keep the water bubbling.

Carefully break in the eggs and cook for about 3-4 minutes. Remove with a slotted spoon and place on top of the rarebit. Sprinkle over the chopped parsley and serve immediately.

Sundried tomato quiches

SERVES

4

PREP AND COOK TIME

40 minutes

INGREDIENTS

250 g | 9 oz | 2 ½ cups plain
(all-purpose) flour

125 g | 4 ½ oz | ½ cup butter

a pinch of salt

1 egg

50 g | 2 oz | ½ cup sundried tomatoes

2 spring onions (scallions), sliced

1 courgette (zucchini), cut into strips

1 clove of garlic, finely chopped

5 eggs, beaten

110 g | 4 oz | 1 cup grated Gruyere cheese

400 ml | 14 fl. oz | 2 cups cream

salt and pepper

Sift the flour into a mixing bowl and stir in the salt. Rub in the butter until the mixture resembles breadcrumbs.

Add the egg and mix to a dough. Wrap in cling film and chill for 30 minutes. Soften the tomatoes briefly in a little warm water, then finely chop.

Heat the oven to 180°C (160° fan) 350F, gas 4. Grease 4 individual tart tins.

Mix the spring onions, courgettes and garlic together. Beat the eggs with the cheese and cream. Season with salt and pepper.

Roll out the dough onto a floured surface and line the tart tins. Prick the bases and bake for 5 minutes. Remove from the oven and allow to cool slightly.

Spread the vegetables over the base of the pastry cases. Pour in the cheese filling and sprinkle with the chopped tomatoes. Bake for 15-20 minutes until the filling is bubbling.

Red pepper soup

SERVES

4

PREP AND COOK TIME

55 minutes

INGREDIENTS

25 g | 1 oz butter

4 red peppers, chopped

1 onion, chopped

3 cloves of garlic, finely chopped

750 ml | 26 fl. oz | 3 cups vegetable stock

100 ml | 3 ½ fl. oz cream

salt and freshly ground black pepper

To garnish:

black and white peppercorns, lightly crushed

baguette slices, to serve

Melt the butter in a large saucepan. Add the peppers, onion and garlic and cook gently for 5-10 minutes, until soft.

Pour in the stock, stirring well, then reduce the heat and simmer for 30 minutes. Pour the soup into a blender and purée until smooth.

Return to the saucepan and stir in the cream. Season the pan to taste with salt and pepper. Heat until piping hot. Pour into bowls and sprinkle with crushed peppercorns.

Cheese and tuna melts

SERVES

4

PREP AND COOK TIME

15 minutes

INGREDIENTS

400 g | 14 oz canned tuna, drained

4 spring onions (scallions), chopped

60g | 2 oz mayonnaise

salt and pepper

4 slices bread

225 g | 8 oz | 1 cup Cheddar cheese, grated

1 tbsp chopped chives

2 tbsp sweetcorn

Set the grill to preheat on the highest setting.

Flake the tuna into a bowl and mix in the spring onions, mayonnaise and sweetcorn and season with salt and pepper.

Toast the bread under the grill until browned on both sides. Spread the tuna mixture on top and scatter over the cheese. Grill the slices until the cheese is bubbling.

Garnish with chives and cucumber slices.

Vegetable quiche

SERVES

4

PREP AND COOK TIME

55 minutes

INGREDIENTS

200 g | 7 oz | 2 cups plain (all-purpose) flour

50 g | 1 ½ oz | ½ cup butter

300 g | 11 oz | 1 ½ cups feta

2 tbsp oil

1 onion, finely chopped

1 clove of garlic, finely chopped

1 red pepper, diced

2 green asparagus spears, halved, lengthways

2 tbsp olive oil

125 g | 4 ½ oz | 1 cup grated cheese

3 eggs

150 ml | 5 fl. oz | 1 cup milk

1 tsp dried oregano

½ courgette (zucchini), sliced

100 g | 3 ½ oz broccoli florets

2 tomatoes, quartered and seeds removed

salt and pepper

3 tbsp breadcrumbs

sage leaves

Put the flour into a mixing bowl and rub in the butter until the mixture resembles breadcrumbs. Add the salt and 200 g of the feta. Knead together to form a smooth dough then wrap in cling film and leave to chill for 30 minutes.

Heat the oven to 200°C (180° fan) 400F, gas 6.
Grease a 28 cm/ 11 " flan tin or dish.

Heat the oil in a frying pan, and then gently cook the onions, garlic and peppers for 3 minutes. Cook the asparagus, courgettes and broccoli in boiling, salted water for 8 minutes, then drain and leave to cool.

Mix the grated cheese, remaining feta, eggs, milk and oregano.

Roll out the dough on a lightly floured surface, a little larger than the dish. Line the greased dish with the dough. Sprinkle the breadcrumbs over the base. Pour in the cheese and egg mixture followed by the prepared vegetables.

Bake for 30 minutes until piping hot. Garnish with sage leaves.

Haddock pie

SERVES

4

PREP AND COOK TIME

1 hour 15 minutes

INGREDIENTS

450 ml | 16 fl. oz | 2 cups milk

150 ml | 5 fl. oz | ⅔ cup cream

2 bay leaves

a pinch of grated nutmeg

450 g | 1 lb smoked haddock

50 g | 2 oz | ¼ cup butter

1 onion, finely chopped

50 g | 2 oz | ½ cup plain (all-purpose) flour

1 tsp chopped thyme

2 tbsp chopped parsley

2 cherry tomatoes, chopped

225 g | 8 oz prawns

500 g | 1 lb potatoes

250 g | 9 oz parsnips

grated nutmeg, salt and pepper

30 g | 1 oz butter

50 ml | 2 fl. oz milk

25 g | 1 oz | ¼ cup grated Parmesan cheese

Heat the oven to 200°C (180° fan) 400F, gas 6 and grease a pie dish with butter.

For the filling, put the milk, cream, bay leaves and nutmeg in a saucepan and allow it to simmer. Add the smoked haddock and poach for 6-8 minutes. Cool slightly, then remove the fish and flake the smoked haddock, then set it aside. Strain the cooking liquor.

Melt the butter in a pan, add the onion and cook for 5 minutes until the onion has softened. Stir in the flour and thyme and cook for 2 minutes. Gradually whisk in the strained poaching liquor. Simmer gently for 5 minutes.

Add the parsley and stir in the tomatoes and flaked fish and season to taste with salt and pepper. Pour the fish mixture into the dish and allow it to cool. Fold in the prawns.

Put the potatoes and parsnips in a pan and cover with cold water. Add a pinch of salt, cover and increase the heat to boiling point. Cook for 25 minutes until tender. Drain and mash with the butter, milk and season with salt, pepper and nutmeg.

Spoon the mashed potatoes and parsnips on top of the fish and fluff with a fork. Sprinkle the cheese over the potatoes. Bake for 35 minutes until bubbling and golden and serve immediately.

Tomato and goat's cheese tarte tatin

SERVES

4

PREP AND COOK TIME

1 hour 40 minutes

INGREDIENTS

250 g | 9 oz | 2 ½ cups plain (all-purpose) flour

1 tsp salt

80 ml | 3 fl. oz | ⅓ cup olive oil

2 tbsp lukewarm water

1 egg

For the topping:

400 g | 14 oz firm, ripe cherry tomatoes, halved

110 g | 4 oz goat's cheese

4 cloves of garlic, finely chopped

60 ml | 2 fl. oz olive oil

salt and pepper

Heat the oven to 220°C (200° fan) 425F, gas 7.

Mix the flour, salt, olive oil, water and egg to a smooth dough. Cover the dough and rest it for an hour at room temperature.

Knead the dough and roll it out between two layers of grease-proof paper into a thin round.

Heat the olive oil in a frying pan and fry the garlic until softened. Arrange the tomatoes in the pan and crumble over the cheese. Sprinkle the garlic on top and season with salt and pepper.

Brush with a little more olive oil and place the dough on top of the tomatoes pressing down slightly. Bake for 25 minutes until the dough is golden brown and crisp. To serve, allow the tarte tatin to cool for a few minutes then gently turn it out onto a plate, and slice.

Cheese scones

MAKES

12

PREP AND COOK TIME

20 minutes

INGREDIENTS

250 g | 9 oz | 2 ¼ cups plain (all-purpose) flour

a pinch of salt

1 tsp cream of tartar

½ tsp bicarbonate of soda (baking soda)

a pinch of cayenne pepper

50 g | 2 oz | ¼ cup butter

75 g | 2 ½ oz | ¾ cup Cheddar cheese, grated

1 egg, beaten

150 ml | 5 fl. oz | ⅔ cup milk

Heat the oven to 220°C (200° fan) 425F, gas 7 and grease a baking tray with a little oil.

Sift the flour, salt, cream of tartar, bicarbonate of soda and cayenne into a mixing bowl. Rub the butter in until the mixture resembles breadcrumbs.

Stir in the cheese, followed by the egg and enough milk to form a very soft dough. Turn the dough out onto a floured surface and roll out to a 2 cm / 1 ¾ " thickness. Cut out rounds with a 3 ½ cm / 1 ½ " cutter.

Place the rounds on the baking tray and bake for 8-10 minutes until golden.

Minestrone soup

SERVES

4

PREP AND COOK TIME

1 hour

INGREDIENTS

45 ml | 1 ½ fl. oz olive oil

1 stick celery, diced

1 onion, diced

1 courgette (zucchini), diced

4 cloves of garlic, finely chopped

2 carrots, diced

1 tsp tomato purée

800 ml | 28 fl. oz | 3 ½ cups vegetable stock

250 g | 9 oz potatoes, peeled and diced

50 g | 2 oz pancetta, diced

400 g | 14 oz tomatoes, peeled and diced

250 g | 9 oz canned white beans, drained

salt and pepper

sprinkling of Parmesan cheese

Heat the oil in a large pan and fry the celery, onion, courgette, garlic and carrots briefly. Stir in the tomato purée, stock, potatoes and pancetta.

Add the tomatoes and simmer for 30 minutes. Add the beans and simmer for a further 10 minutes, if necessary add more stock. Season to taste with salt and pepper. Sprinkle Parmesan cheese on top and serve.

Leek and goat's cheese tart

SERVES

4

PREP AND COOK TIME

45 minutes

INGREDIENTS

500 g | 1 lb puff pastry

2 tbsp oil

6 leeks, thinly sliced

200 g | 7 oz goat's cheese, crumbled

300 ml | 11 fl. oz | 1 ½ cups single cream

2 large eggs

2 large egg yolks

black pepper

grated nutmeg

a pinch of salt

marjoram leaves

Heat the oven to 200°C (180° fan) 400F, gas 6. Line a baking tray with greaseproof baking paper.

Roll out the pastry and cut out a 24 cm x 36 cm / 10 " x 14 " rectangle. Place it onto the baking tray. Using the tip of a sharp knife, mark a border inside about 1 ½ cm / ½ " from the edge.

Heat the oil in a frying pan and cook the leeks for 10 minutes, until soft but not coloured. Remove them from the pan and spoon over the pastry base. Scatter the cheese over the leeks.

Whisk the cream, eggs and egg yolks together. Season with pepper, nutmeg, and salt. Pour over the cheese and leeks.

Bake for 20-25 minutes until golden. Garnish with marjoram and serve warm.

Potato and bacon quiches

SERVES

4

PREP AND COOK TIME

1 hour 45 minutes

INGREDIENTS

200 g | 7 oz | 1 ¾ cups plain (all-purpose) flour

½ tsp fast action yeast

½ tsp sugar

a pinch of salt

50 ml | 2 fl. oz vegetable oil

125 ml | 4 ½ fl. oz | ½ cup lukewarm water

For the filling:

1 leek, thinly sliced

800 g | 1 ¾ lbs potatoes, thinly sliced

150 g | 5 oz | ¾ cup cream cheese (soft cheese)

250 ml | 9 fl. oz | 1 cup cream

50 g | 2 oz | ½ cup grated Parmesan cheese

3 eggs

salt and pepper

grated nutmeg

60 g | 2 oz smoked bacon, cut into strips

For the pastry, place the flour in a mixing bowl and sprinkle with the yeast, sugar, salt and oil. Add the water and knead to a smooth dough. Cover the dough and leave it to rise in a warm place for 30 minutes.

Heat the oven to 200°C (180° fan) 400F, gas 6 and grease 4 individual quiche tins with butter.

Roll out the dough and line the tins, pressing it down. Spread the potato and leek slices on the pastry base.

Beat the cream cheese with the cream, Parmesan and eggs and season with salt, pepper and nutmeg. Pour the mixture over the potatoes and leeks to cover them. Sprinkle with bacon strips.

Bake for about 35 minutes until golden brown.

Buckwheat pancakes

MAKES

8

PREP AND COOK TIME

20 minutes

INGREDIENTS

300 ml | 11 fl. oz | 1 ⅓ cups milk

55 g | 2 oz | ½ cup wholemeal flour

55 g | 2 oz | ½ cup buckwheat flour

1 egg

a pinch of salt

1 tsp vegetable oil

Mix the milk, egg, salt and oil in a mixing bowl.

Gradually beat in both flours, mixing constantly until a smooth batter is formed. Leave the batter to rest for 30 minutes.

Heat a little oil in a frying pan until very hot. Pour in $\frac{1}{8}$ of the batter and cook for 1-2 minutes on each side, until golden.

Remove the pancake from the pan and place on a sheet of greaseproof baking paper and keep warm while repeating the process with the remaining batter to make 8 pancakes.

These pancakes can be served sweet or savoury.

Vegetable tart

SERVES

4

PREP AND COOK TIME

1 hour 20 minutes

INGREDIENTS

250 g | 9 oz plain (all-purpose) flour

a pinch of salt

110 g | 4 oz butter, cubed

55 ml | 2 fl. oz cold water

For the filling:

45 ml | 1 ½ fl. oz oil

2 red onions, sliced

1 clove of garlic, finely chopped

2 red peppers, diced

1 small courgette (zucchini), sliced

100 g | 3 ½ oz cherry tomatoes

100 g | 3 ½ oz button mushrooms, halved

1-2 tbsp each of oregano, basil and thyme

salt and pepper

For the pastry, put the flour in a mixing bowl and rub in the butter until the mixture resembles breadcrumbs. Stir in the salt and a tablespoon of water at a time and mix to a smooth dough. Wrap the dough in cling film and chill for 30 minutes.

Heat the oven to 200°C (180° fan) 400F, gas 6 and grease a rectangular bevel-edged tart tin.

For the filling, heat 2 tablespoons of the oil in a frying pan and gently cook the onion, garlic, courgette and pepper over a medium heat for 3 minutes.

Mix the contents of the pan with the tomatoes, mushrooms and herbs and season to taste with salt and pepper.

Roll out the dough slightly larger than the tin and line the tin with the dough, overlapping the edges.

Spoon the vegetables onto the pastry base. Drizzle with the remaining oil and bake for 30 minutes until the vegetables are tender.

Bacon and parmesan scones

MAKES

10

PREP AND COOK TIME

30 minutes

INGREDIENTS

110 g | 4 oz | ½ cup diced bacon

225 g | 8 oz | 2 cups self-raising flour

2 tsp baking powder

a pinch of salt

25 g | 1 oz | ⅛ cup butter

55 g | 2 oz | ¼ cup Parmesan cheese, grated

150 ml | 5 fl. oz milk

1 egg, beaten

Heat the oven to 200°C (180° fan) 400F, gas 6 and lightly grease a baking tray with oil. Heat a frying pan and cook the bacon without adding any oil or butter, until browned.

Sift the flour, baking powder and salt into a mixing bowl. Rub the butter in, until the mixture resembles breadcrumbs and then stir in the grated cheese and bacon.

Make a well in the centre of the mixture and pour in just enough milk to form a soft but not sticky dough. Turn the dough out onto a floured surface and knead lightly until smooth.

Roll or pat the dough out to a thickness of 2 cm / 1 " and cut out 10 rounds with a cutter.

Place the rounds on the baking tray and brush the tops lightly with a little beaten egg. Bake the scones for about 15 minutes until golden brown.

Beetroot chutney

MAKES

makes: 2 x 500 g jars

PREP AND COOK TIME

55 minutes

INGREDIENTS

400 g | 1 lb beetroot

salt

200 ml | 7 fl. oz | ⅞ cup red wine vinegar

50 ml | 2 fl. oz dry red wine

3 cloves

6 allspice berries

150 g | 5 oz onions, chopped

200 g | 7 oz | 2 cups diced cooking apples

20 g | ½ oz fresh ginger, finely chopped

75 g | 2 ½ oz raisins

75 g | 2 ½ oz light brown sugar

Cook the beetroot in a pan of boiling, salted water for 20 minutes. Drain and cut it into small cubes.

Put the red wine vinegar, wine, cloves and allspice in a pan and increase the heat to boiling point. Add the onions and apples and simmer for 10 minutes.

Add the beetroot, ginger, raisins and brown sugar and simmer for a further 15 minutes. Remove the cloves and allspice and season with salt to taste.

Pour the chutney into sterilised jars and seal tightly. Store in a cool, dark place and consume within a week of opening.

Homemade meals

Lemon and garlic roasted chicken

SERVES

4

PREP AND COOK TIME

1 hour 40 minutes

INGREDIENTS

1 large free range chicken

olive oil

1 bunch fresh thyme, chopped

4-6 unwaxed lemons

salt and freshly ground pepper

1-2 tbsp honey

6 cloves of garlic, halved

6 shallots, halved

Heat the oven to 180°C (160° fan) 350F, gas 4.

Halve and squeeze the juice from 1 lemon. Slice another lemon and mix it with a little olive oil, half the thyme, salt and pepper.

Stuff the chicken with the sliced lemon and herbs.

Mix the lemon juice with the honey, 1 tablesppon of olive oil, salt and pepper and brush the chicken with the mixture.

Halve the remaining lemons and place them in the roasting dish. Put the garlic cloves and shallots into the dish. Place the chicken in the dish, scatter the rest of the thyme on top of the chicken and cook for 40 minutes per kg / 2 ½ lbs, plus an extra 20 minutes, until golden and cooked through.

Insert a skewer into the chicken between the leg and thigh, the juices should run clear with no trace of pink when the chicken is cooked.

Beef ragout

SERVES

SERVES

4

PREP AND COOK TIME

3 hours 20 minutes

INGREDIENTS

30 ml | 1 fl. oz oil

750 g | 1 ½ lb stewing steak, diced

100 g | 3 ½ oz | ½ cup diced streaky bacon

300 g | 11 oz small onions

4 parsnips, quartered

4 carrots, chopped

2 cloves of garlic, crushed

55 ml | 2 fl. oz brandy

500 ml | 18 fl. oz | 2 cups red wine

salt and pepper

2 sprigs thyme

Heat the oven to 150°C (130° fan) 300F, gas 2.

Heat the oil in a large frying pan and brown the stewing steak. Place into a baking dish. Add the bacon, onions, parsnips, carrots and garlic to the pan and cook briefly until just browned. Place into the baking dish.

Pour in the brandy and red wine. Season to taste with salt and pepper and stir everything together. Cover and cook for 3-3 ½ hours until the meat is very tender. Garnish with thyme sprigs to serve.

Lancashire hotpot

SERVES

4

PREP AND COOK TIME

1 hour 50 minutes

INGREDIENTS

600 g | 1 ¼ lbs waxy potatoes,

peeled and thinly sliced

1 onion, diced

2 carrots, diced

2 cloves of garlic, sliced

1 medium celeriac (celery root), diced

500 g | 1 lb braising lamb, cubed

750 ml | 26 fl. oz | 3 cups lamb stock

30 g | 1 oz butter

2 tbsp marjoram

2 tsp fresh rosemary

Heat the oven to 200°C (180° fan) 400F, gas 6. Butter a casserole dish.

Layer the ingredients in the casserole dish, beginning with a layer of potatoes, then vegetables and then meat. Season the layer with salt, pepper, garlic and herbs between layers. Finish with a neat layer of potatoes and season again.

Pour the stock over, cover and cook for 1 ½ hours until the meat is tender. Brush the potatoes with the butter 20 minutes before the end of the cooking time and cook uncovered to brown the potatoes.

Herbed rib of beef

SERVES

4

PREP AND COOK TIME

1 hour 40 minutes

INGREDIENTS

1 kg | 2 ¼ lb boneless rib of beef, rolled and tied

45 ml | 1 ½ fl. oz oil

2 tsp salt

2 tsp peppercorns, lightly crushed

3 tsp chopped thyme

3 tsp chopped sage

3 tsp chopped chives

3 tsp chopped parsley

Heat the oven to 180°C (160° fan) 350F, gas 4.

Rub some oil into the beef. Mix the salt, peppercorns and herbs together. Spoon the herb mixture onto the beef and spread it evenly to cover all sides.

Put the remaining oil in a large roasting tin and add the rib of beef. Roast for 1 ½ hours for medium, deduct 15 minutes for rare, and add 15-20 minutes to the cooking time if you prefer meat well done.

Leave the meat to rest for 10 minutes before carving.

Cottage pie

SERVES

4

PREP AND COOK TIME

1 hour

INGREDIENTS

1 tbsp oil

1 large onion, chopped

2 carrots, chopped

550 g | 1 ¼ lb minced beef

60 ml | 2 fl. oz Worcestershire sauce

400 ml | 14 fl. oz | 2 cups beef stock

2 tbsp tomato purée

salt and ground black pepper

1 kg | 2 ¼ lb potatoes, peeled and diced

75 g | 2 ½ oz butter

grated nutmeg

Heat the oil in a large pan. Add the onion and carrots and cook over a medium heat for 5 minutes until soft. Add the minced beef and cook for 3 minutes until brown. Add the Worcestershire sauce, stock and tomato purée.

Cover and simmer for 30 minutes. Season to taste with salt and pepper. Heat the oven to 190°C (170° fan) 375F, gas 5. Grease 4 small baking dishes.

Put the potatoes in a pan and cover with cold water. Increase the heat to boiling point and cook for 15 minutes, until tender. Drain and add the butter. Mash together and season to taste with nutmeg, salt and pepper.

Spoon the meat into the dishes. Spoon the mashed potatoes on top and cook for 30 minutes until the potatoes are lightly browned and the filling is piping hot.

Roast pork

SERVES

4-6

PREP AND COOK TIME

2 hours 10 minutes

INGREDIENTS

1 ½ kg | 3 ¼ lbs pork shoulder, deboned

vegetable oil

2 tbsp chopped thyme

6 cloves of garlic, crushed

salt and pepper

Heat the oven to 190°C (170° fan) 375F, gas 5.

Score the pork rind deeply with a sharp knife, making a criss-cross pattern. Brush the rind with a little oil.

Mix the salt, pepper, thyme and garlic together and rub well into the rind.

Place the meat in a roasting tin and cook for 30 minutes.

Reduce the oven temperature to 180°C (160° fan) 350F, gas 4 and cook for a further 1 ½ hours, until the pork is cooked and the fat is crackling. Allow the pork to rest for 15 minutes before carving.

Sausage
and mash

SERVES

4

PREP AND COOK TIME

45 minutes

INGREDIENTS

1 tbsp butter

1 tsp sugar

4 onions, thinly sliced

150 ml | 5 fl. oz | 1 cup red wine

salt and pepper

1 tbsp oil

8 sausages

1 kg | 2 lb potatoes, peeled and cubed

50 g | 2 oz | ½ cup butter

200 ml | 7 fl. oz | 1 cup cream

salt

grated nutmeg

Put the potatoes in a large pan of salted water and increase the heat to boiling point. Cook for 25 minutes until tender.

Heat the butter in a frying pan, add the sugar and cook until lightly browned. Add the onions and cook gently, then stir in the wine and simmer. Season to taste with salt and pepper.

Heat the oil in a frying pan and cook the sausages for 15-20 minutes until browned and cooked through.

Drain and mash with a potato masher. Heat the butter and cream and mix into the mashed potato. Beat well until smooth and season to taste with salt and nutmeg.

Spring greens risotto

SERVES

4

PREP AND COOK TIME

35 minutes

INGREDIENTS

50 g | 2 oz broad beans, podded

80 g | 3 oz | 1 cup garden peas

50 g | 2 oz French beans, sliced

50 g | 2 oz asparagus tips

110 g | 4 oz | ½ cup butter

3 shallots, finely chopped

300 g | 11 oz | 1 ¾ cups risotto rice

120 ml | 4 fl. oz | ½ cup dry white wine

1 l | 35 fl. oz | 4 cups vegetable stock

salt and black pepper

2 tbsp fresh mint, chopped

grated Parmesan cheese

Melt 75 g of the butter in a large shallow pan, add the shallots and fry gently until softened. Add the rice and cook for a few moments to absorb the butter.

Add the wine and cook over a medium heat for 5-10 minutes until evaporated.

Season the pan with pepper. Add a ladleful of stock and cook until absorbed. Cook for a further 15-20 minutes in total, adding the stock, a ladleful at a time, stirring constantly until the stock has been absorbed before adding more stock.

Add the asparagus tips, beans and peas and cook for 2-3 minutes. Stir in the mint and the remaining butter. Spoon the risotto into serving dishes and sprinkle with Parmesan cheese.

Chicken and mushroom pie

SERVES

4

PREP AND COOK TIME

1 hour

INGREDIENTS

60 ml | 2 fl. oz oil

4 boneless, skinless chicken breasts, sliced

200 g | 7 oz chestnut mushrooms, quartered

1 onion, chopped

1 clove of garlic, chopped

30 g | 1 oz flour

100 ml | 3 ½ fl. oz white wine

200 ml | 7 fl. oz | 1 cup chicken stock

200 ml | 7 fl. oz | 1 cup cream

3 egg yolks

3 tbsp chopped parsley

salt

freshly ground pepper

grated nutmeg

300 g | 11 oz puff pastry

1 tbsp water

Heat the oven to 200°C (180° fan) 400F, gas 6. Grease a pie dish or baking dish.

Heat 2 tablespoons of oil in a frying pan and lightly brown the chicken. Remove from the heat and set aside. Heat the remaining oil and cook the mushrooms until tender. Remove from the pan and set aside with the chicken.

Add the onions and garlic to the pan and cook gently until translucent. Stir in the flour and wine and cook gently until slightly thickened. Stir in the stock and half the cream. Simmer until creamy and slightly reduced, then return the chicken and mushrooms to the pan and cook briefly. Remove from the heat.

Mix 2 egg yolks with the remaining cream and stir into the chicken mixture. Add the parsley and season to taste with salt, pepper and nutmeg. Spoon into the baking dish.

Roll out the puff pastry and cut out a circle to cover the pie dish. Place it on top of the filling and press the edges down firmly. Whisk the remaining egg yolk with water and brush over the pastry.

Cut a slit in the centre of the pastry and bake for 20 minutes, until the pastry rises and browns. Serve immediately.

Toad in the hole

SERVES

4

PREP AND COOK TIME

55 minutes

INGREDIENTS

30 ml | 1 fl. oz oil

450 g | 1 lb pork sausages

225 g | 8 oz | 2 cups plain (all-purpose) flour

a pinch of salt

2 eggs

600 ml | 21 fl. oz | 2 ½ cups milk

Heat the oven to 220°C (200° fan) 425F, gas 7.

Heat a tablespoon of oil in a frying pan and fry the sausages for 5 minutes until browned on all sides.

Heat the remaining oil in a large baking dish or roasting tin in the oven until very hot.

Put the flour and salt into a mixing bowl and make a well in the centre. Break in the eggs and gradually work in half the milk, beating well until smooth. Beat in the rest of the milk.

Place the sausages in the dish and pour over the batter. Bake for 30-35 minutes until risen. Serve with mashed potato and green beans.

Pot au feu

SERVES

4

PREP AND COOK TIME

1 hour

INGREDIENTS

1 chicken, cut into 8 pieces

salt and pepper

60 ml | 2 fl. oz olive oil

1 tbsp thyme

2 bay leaves

1 clove of garlic, finely diced

200 ml | 7 fl. oz | ⅞ cup chicken stock

8 spring onion (scallions), chopped

250 g | 9 oz | 2 cups green asparagus, trimmed

200 g | 7 oz small carrots, washed

400 g | 14 oz small potatoes, scrubbed

Season the chicken pieces with salt and pepper. Heat the oil in a large saucepan and brown the chicken pieces on all sides.

Add the thyme, bay leaves and garlic, stir briefly with the chicken and then add the stock.

Simmer gently for 30 minutes.

Add the prepared vegetables and simmer for a further 20 minutes and season to taste with salt and pepper.

Shepherd's pie

SERVES

4

PREP AND COOK TIME

1 hour 15 minutes

INGREDIENTS

600 g | 1 ¼ lb potatoes, peeled and diced

salt and pepper

30 g | 1 oz butter

50 ml | 2 fl. oz milk

grated nutmeg

1 egg, beaten

2 carrots, diced

1 small turnip, chopped

1 tbsp oil

600 g | 1 ¼ lb minced lamb

1 onion, chopped

150 g | 5 oz | 1 cup peas

50 ml | 2 fl. oz lamb or vegetable stock

1 tbsp tomato purée

Put the potatoes in a pan and cover with cold water. Add a pinch of salt, cover and heat to boiling point. Cook for 25 minutes until tender.

Drain the potatoes and mash with the butter and milk. Season with salt, pepper and nutmeg and beat in the egg.

Blanch the carrots and turnip in boiling, salted water for 8 minutes. Drain and set aside. Heat the oven to 200°C (180° fan) 400F, gas 6. Grease a baking dish with a little butter.

Heat the oil in a frying pan over a medium heat and add the minced lamb. Stir until browned, then stir in the onion, peas, stock and tomato purée. Put into the baking dish.

Spread the mashed potatoes over the meat and bake for 25-30 minutes until the potatoes are browned and the filling is piping hot.

Vegetable stew

SERVES

4

PREP AND COOK TIME

45 minutes

INGREDIENTS

12 small new potatoes

½ tsp salt

600 ml | 21 fl. oz | 2 ½ cups vegetable stock

100 g | 3 ½ oz mangetout

100 g | 3 ½ oz French beans, sliced

60 g | 2 oz peas

60 g | 2 oz sweetcorn

8 asparagus spears

2 tbsp flatleaf parsley, chopped

4 spring onions (scallions), sliced

4 green olives, pitted and sliced

Put the potatoes and salt in a large pan and pour in the stock. Increase the heat to boiling point and cook for 5 minutes.

Add the remaining vegetables to the pan, and increase the heat to boiling point. Cover and cook gently for 15-20 minutes until the vegetables are tender. If the stew becomes too dry, add a little more stock or water. If you want a thicker consistency, add a tablespoon of cornflour mixed with a little water for the last 3 minutes of the cooking time.

Spoon into serving bowls. Garnish using the parsley, spring onions and olives.

Macaroni cheese

SERVES

4

PREP AND COOK TIME

35 minutes

INGREDIENTS

225 g | 8 oz | 2 cups grated cheese

50 g | 2 oz | ½ cup grated Parmesan cheese

50 g | 2 oz | 1 cup breadcrumbs

a pinch of salt

300 g | 11 oz | 3 cups macaroni

700 ml | 25 fl. oz | 3 cups milk

50 g | 2 oz | ½ cup butter

50 g | 2 oz | ½ cup plain (all-purpose) flour

1 tsp Dijon mustard

Heat the oven to 190°C (170° fan) 375F, gas 5. Grease a baking dish with butter, 30 cm x 20 cm x 5 ½ cm / 12 " x 8 " x 2 ".

Mix 25 g of the cheese and 20 g of the Parmesan with the breadcrumbs. Mix the remaining cheese together and set aside.

Heat a large pot of water to boiling point. Add the salt and macaroni to the pot, leave it to simmer for 8 minutes, or cook according to the packet instructions. Stir occasionally to prevent it sticking.

Warm the milk separately and then melt the butter in a saucepan and stir in the flour. Cook for 1 minute, stirring, and then remove from the heat. Pour in 200 ml of the warm milk and beat well until smooth. Add another 200 ml of the milk and continue beating until smooth. Pour in the rest of the milk and beat until smooth.

Cook the sauce, stirring, until thickened and smooth. Reduce the heat and leave it to simmer for 4 minutes. Remove from the heat and stir in the cheese and mustard. If the sauce is too thick add a little more milk.

Drain the macaroni in a colander and rinse under running water. Gently coat the macaroni with sauce. Tip the macaroni cheese into the baking dish and scatter the cheese breadcrumbs over the top. Bake for 12-15 minutes.

Heat the grill. Place the baking dish under the grill for 5 minutes to brown the topping. Serve immediately.

Fried chicken

SERVES

4

PREP AND COOK TIME

50 minutes

INGREDIENTS

8 chicken pieces

200 ml | 7 fl. oz | 1 cup milk

200 g | 7 oz | 2 cups self-raising flour

a large pinch of turmeric

½ tsp ground black pepper

½ tsp paprika

1 ½ tsp cayenne pepper

1 ½ tsp garlic salt

120 ml | 4 ½ fl. oz oil

Heat the oven to 200°C (180° fan) 400F, gas 6.

Put the chicken in a bowl and pour the milk over it. Put the flour and spices into a large plastic bag and shake well.

Take 4 chicken pieces out of the milk, shake off any excess and put in the bag of seasoned flour. Close the top of the bag and shake well to coat the chicken. Repeat with the remaining pieces of chicken.

Heat the oil in a large frying pan and fry 4 pieces of chicken at a time on both sides until golden.

Place the chicken in a roasting tin and bake for 30 minutes until cooked.

Seafood pie

SERVES

4

PREP AND COOK TIME

1 hour 25 minutes

INGREDIENTS

600 g | 1 ¼ lb cod or pollock fillet

200 g | 7 oz prawns

30 g | 1 oz butter

1 leek, sliced

40 g | 1 ½ oz | ⅓ cup plain (all-purpose) flour

400 ml | 14 fl. oz | 1 ⅔ cups fish stock

250 ml | 9 fl. oz | 1 cup cream

80 g | 3 oz | ¾ cup grated cheese

2 tbsp fresh parsley, chopped

grated nutmeg

For the mashed potato topping:

200 g | 7 oz floury potatoes

40 ml | 1 ½ fl. oz hot milk

2 tbsp mild mustard

30 g | 1 oz butter

salt

grated nutmeg

Heat the oven to 200°C (180° fan) 400F, gas 6 and lightly grease a large baking dish or 4 individual baking dishes with oil.

Mix the fish and the prawns together and place in the baking dish. Heat the butter in a pan and cook the leek until soft. Stir in the flour, stock and cream and simmer for 10 minutes, stirring continuously until thickened.

Stir in half the cheese and the parsley and season with salt, pepper and nutmeg. Pour the mixture over the fish and bake for 20 minutes.

Cook the potatoes in boiling, salted water for 15-20 minutes until tender. Drain the potatoes and mash them or put them through a potato ricer. Stir in the hot milk, mustard and butter and season with salt and nutmeg.

Spoon the mashed potato on top of the fish mixture in the dish and sprinkle with the remaining cheese. Bake for a further 10-15 minutes until golden on top and the fish mixture is bubbling.

Boeuf bourguignon with tagliatelle

SERVES

4

PREP AND COOK TIME

3 hours

INGREDIENTS

30 ml | 1 fl. oz olive oil

80 g | 3 oz bacon, chopped

750 g | 1 ½ lbs stewing beef, cubed

3 tbsp tomato paste

500 ml | 18 fl. oz | 2 cups red wine

250 ml | 9 fl. oz | 1 cup beef stock

1 tsp chopped thyme

1 bay leaf

salt and pepper

1 tbsp flour

30 ml | 1 fl. oz butter

400 g | 14 oz shallots

400 g | 14 oz button mushrooms

350 g | 12 oz tagliatelle pasta

thyme sprigs

Heat the oven to 150°C (130° fan) 300F, gas 2.

Heat the oil in a flameproof casserole dish and cook the bacon until browned. Add the beef in batches and brown quickly on all sides. Remove the meat and set aside.

Stir the tomato paste into the pan, followed by the wine and stock. Add the bacon, meat, thyme and bay leaf and season to taste with salt and pepper. Cover and cook in the oven for an hour.

Mix the flour with the butter and stir into the casserole with the shallots. Cover and cook for a further hour. Add the mushrooms and cook for a further 30 minutes.

Cook the tagliatelle according to the pack instructions and serve with the Boeuf bourguignon garnished with the thyme.

Sausage hotpot

SERVES

4

PREP AND COOK TIME

45 minutes

INGREDIENTS

800 g | 1 ¾ lbs small pork sausages

1 tbsp olive oil

400 g | 14 oz shallots, quartered

1 clove garlic, finely chopped

1 tbsp sugar

30 ml | 1 fl. oz balsamic vinegar

125 ml | 4 ½ fl. oz | ½ cup chicken stock

600 g | 1 ¼ lbs potatoes, peeled
and thinly sliced

30 g | 1 oz butter

Heat the oven to 220°C (200° fan) 425F, gas 7.

Fry the sausages with a teaspoon of oil in a frying pan for 5 minutes until golden brown and then remove from the heat.

Heat the remaining oil in a shallow, flameproof casserole dish and cook the shallots and garlic over a medium heat until translucent.

Sprinkle in the sugar and allow it to caramelise slightly, deglaze the pan with the vinegar, to reduce the sauce a little and then pour in the stock.

Add the sausages to the shallots, season with salt and pepper and lay the potato slices on top. Cover with a lid and cook for 5 minutes.

Remove the lid, put the butter in small pieces on the potatoes and bake in the oven for about 15 minutes until the potatoes are browned.

Beef and ale pie

SERVES

4

PREP AND COOK TIME

2 hours 25 minutes

INGREDIENTS

salt and pepper

45 ml | 1 ½ fl. oz oil

1 tbsp plain (all-purpose) flour

2 onions, chopped

1 kg | 2 ½ lbs braising steak, diced

220 ml | 8 fl. oz | ⅞ cup dark ale

275 g | 10 oz puff pastry

200 ml | 7 fl. oz | ⅞ cup beef stock

1 tbsp tomato purée

2 bay leaves, crushed

1 egg yolk, beaten

Season the flour with salt and pepper and coat the meat in the seasoned flour.

Heat 2 tablespoons of oil in a large, deep pan and brown the diced steak in batches. Remove the meat from the pan and set aside.

Add the remaining oil to the pan and cook the onions over a medium heat until translucent. Stir in the ale, tomato purée and stock, then add the meat and bay leaves and simmer. Cover the meat and cook on a low heat for 1-1 ½ hours until the meat is tender. Transfer to a pie dish and leave it to cool.

Heat the oven to 200°C (180° fan) 400F, gas 6.

Roll out the pastry and cover the dish, trimming off any excess and pinching the edges so that it adheres to the dish. Lightly brush with the beaten egg yolk.

Make a few small incisions in the pastry and cook for about 20-30 minutes until the pastry is crisp and golden and the filling is piping hot.

Pork chops with mash

SERVES

4

PREP AND COOK TIME

50 minutes

INGREDIENTS

1 tbsp oil

4 pork chops, bone in

6 cloves of garlic

1 kg | 2 ½ lbs potatoes, peeled and chopped

50 g | 2 oz | ¼ cup butter

200 ml | 7 fl. oz | ⅞ cup milk

salt and pepper

grated nutmeg

For the mashed potatoes, put the potatoes in a large pan of salted water and increase the heat to boiling point. Cook for about 25 minutes until tender.

Make 2 cm / 1 " deep cuts all along the fatty side of the chops using a sharp knife, this will help to make the skin crisp. Sprinkle the chops with salt and pepper.

Heat the oil in a frying pan and cook the chops for 6-8 minutes (depending on their thickness) on each side until the fat is crisp and golden and the meat is cooked. Add the whole garlic cloves to the pan and cook for a few minutes until soft and golden.

Drain and mash the potatoes. Heat the butter and milk and mix into the mashed potato. Beat well until smooth and season to taste with salt, pepper and nutmeg.

Spoon the mashed potato into serving dishes and place the chops and garlic cloves on top, serve with fresh greens.

Desserts

Summer pudding

SERVES

4

PREP AND COOK TIME

20 minutes

INGREDIENTS

175 g | 6 oz | 1 cup sugar

100 ml | 3 ½ fl. oz water

½ tsp vanilla extract

100 g | 3 ½ oz | 1 cup blueberries

100 g | 3 ½ oz | ½ cup strawberries, quartered

100 g | 3 ½ oz | 1 cup raspberries

red wine

12 slices white bread, crusts removed

Put the sugar, water and vanilla into a pan and increase the heat to boiling point. Reduce the heat and simmer for 7-8 minutes, then add the berries and wine. Remove the pan from the heat.

Cut the bread into rounds to fit 4 individual dariole moulds or ramekins. Place a round of bread in the base of each mould and spoon in a layer of the warm fruit and the juices. Repeat the layers ending with bread on the top. Spoon over any remaining juice.

Press down to pack the bread and berries into the moulds. Cover them with cling film and leave to chill in the refrigerator overnight.

Remove the puddings from the moulds, place onto serving plates and serve with cream.

White chocolate ice-cream cake

SERVES

4

PREP AND COOK TIME

50 minutes

INGREDIENTS

60 ml | 2 fl. oz warm water

50 g | 2 oz | ½ cup sugar

1 tsp vanilla extract

2 egg whites

80 g | 3 oz | ½ cup flour

300 g | 11 oz white chocolate

4 eggs

60 ml | 2 fl. oz cold water

1 tbsp orange liqueur

600 ml | 21 fl. oz | 2 ½ cups cream

600 g | 1 ½ lbs | 5 cups mixed berries

Heat the oven to 190°C (170° fan) 375F, gas 5. Line a cake tin with greaseproof paper.

Beat 2 of the egg yolks with the warm water, sugar and vanilla extract until thick and foamy. Whisk the 2 egg whites until they form stiff peaks.

Fold the beaten egg whites into the egg yolk mixture. Sift the flour over the mixture and fold in. Spread the mixture evenly in the tin and bake for 10-12 minutes until golden. Leave to cool in the tin.

Melt the chocolate in a heatproof bowl over a pan of simmering water. Whisk the remaining eggs with the cold water in a heatproof bowl over a pan of simmering water until foamy. Stir in the chocolate and orange liqueur. Remove from the pan and allow to cool.

Whisk the cream until thick and fold into the chocolate mixture. Spread the filling evenly on the sponge base and place in the freezer for 4 hours.

Remove the cake from the tin, allow it to thaw briefly and serve decorated with berries.

Créme bruleé

SERVES
4-6

PREP AND COOK TIME
50 minutes

INGREDIENTS

250 ml | 9 fl. oz | 1 cup milk

250 ml | 9 fl. oz | 1 cup cream

1 vanilla pod (bean)

3 eggs

3 egg yolks

1 tsp of grated lemon zest

75 g | 2 ½ oz | ½ cup sugar

1 tbsp cornflour (cornstarch)

sugar, for sprinkling

Heat the oven to 200°C (180° fan) 400F, gas 6. Grease 4-6 ramekins.

Scrape the seeds out of the vanilla pod and place both into a pan with the milk and all but 2 tablespoons of cream. Increase the heat to boiling point.

Mix the cornflour with the remaining cream, stir into the hot milk and briefly increase the heat to boiling point. Remove the pan from the heat.

Beat the eggs and egg yolks with the lemon zest and sugar until creamy. Stir into the hot milk. Strain through a sieve into the ramekins.

Place the ramekins in a roasting tin or large baking dish and add enough hot water to come halfway up the ramekins. Cover with tin foil and bake for 35 minutes, until the créme has set. Leave to cool, then chill in the refrigerator for at least 2 hours.

Before serving:
Heat the grill. Sprinkle sugar onto the créme and place under the hot grill until the sugar bubbles and caramelises. Alternatively you may wish to caramelise the sugar using a blowtorch.

Walnut cake

SERVES

8-12

PREP AND COOK TIME

1 hour 5 minutes

INGREDIENTS

325 g | 11 ½ oz | 1 ½ cup sugar

9 eggs, separated

a pinch of salt

120 g | 4 oz | ½ cup butter, melted

200 g | 7 oz | 2 cups flour

150 g | 5 oz | 1 ½ cups ground walnuts

5 eggs, whole

250 g | 9 oz | 1 cup butter

60 ml | 2 fl. oz whisky

To decorate:

8 walnut halves

Heat the oven to 180°C (160° fan) 350F, gas 4. Grease a pair of 20 cm / 8 " sandwich tins.

Whisk 225 g of the sugar and egg yolks until fluffy. Whisk the egg whites and a pinch of salt until stiff. Stir $1/3$ of the egg whites into the sugar mixture. Gently stir in the melted butter, flour and ground walnuts until smooth. Fold in the remaining egg whites until blended.

Spoon into the tins and bake for 40-45 minutes until golden. Remove from the oven and allow it to cool in the tins for a few minutes, then place on a wire rack to cool completely.

Whisk the eggs, remaining sugar and a pinch of salt in a bowl, over a pan of simmering water, until thick and creamy. Remove from the heat and beat until cold.

Beat the butter until very soft and creamy. Gradually beat in the egg yolk mixture with the whisky until smooth.

Sandwich the cakes together using half of the whisky cream in the middle. Spread the remaining whisky cream on top and decorate with walnut halves.

Rhubarb and raspberry crumble

SERVES

4

PREP AND COOK TIME

35 minutes

INGREDIENTS

500 g | 1 lb rhubarb, cubed

200 g | 7 oz | 1 ½ cups raspberries

½ lemon, juice

150 g | 5 oz | sugar

150 g | 5 oz | 2 cups rolled oats

60 g | 2 oz | 1 cup plain (all-purpose) flour

110 g | 4 oz | ½ cup butter, melted

1 tsp ground cinnamon

Heat the oven to 180°C (160° fan) 350F, gas 4. Grease a baking dish with butter.

Mix the rhubarb, raspberries, sugar and lemon juice together and pour into the baking dish.

Mix the remaining ingredients together until crumbly. Spread over the fruit in the baking dish. Bake for 20-25 minutes until the rhubarb is tender and the crumble is golden.

Sticky toffee pudding

SERVES

4

PREP AND COOK TIME

1 hour 30 minutes

INGREDIENTS

For the puddings:

125 ml | 4 ½ fl. oz | ½ cup cream

½ vanilla pod

50 g | 2 oz | butter

80 g | 3 oz | 1 cup self-raising flour

4 egg whites

3 egg yolks

50 g | 2 oz | ground walnuts

50 g | 2 oz | sugar

butter, for the basins

50 g | 2 oz | ground almonds, for the bowls

For the sauce:

60 g | 2 oz butter

100 g | 3 ½ oz | ½ cup sugar

50 g | 2 oz | ½ cup chopped pecan nuts

50 g | 2 oz | ½ cup chopped walnuts

100 ml | 3 ½ fl. oz water

Heat the oven to 190°C (170° fan) 375F, gas 5. Grease four individual, ovenproof bowls.

Heat the cream in a pan. Slit the vanilla pod lengthwise and scrape the seeds into the cream. Heat 3 tablespoons of butter in another pan and stir in the flour. Add the cream mixture and heat, stirring, until the mixture forms a ball. Remove from the heat, leave it to cool slightly and stir in 1 egg white. Gradually stir in the egg yolks and the walnuts, then leave it to cool.

Beat the remaining egg whites until they form soft peaks, add 50 g of the sugar and continue beating until firm and glossy. Carefully fold the beaten egg whites into the flour mixture.

Spoon the mixture into the bowls. Seal the bowls with tin foil, then stand them in a roasting tin or baking dish and fill with water to a depth of 3 cm / 1 " below the rim of the bowls. Put into the oven and cook the puddings for 50 minutes, or until cooked through. Melt the butter and sugar in a pan over a medium heat. Stir over the heat until the sugar begins to caramelise. Add the pecans and walnuts to the pan as soon as the sugar begins to brown. Caramelise the nuts briefly, then slowly stir in the water and cook until the sauce has a syrup consistency. Remove the caramel and nut sauce from the heat.

Remove the puddings from the bowls. Spoon the nuts from the toffee sauce on top of the puddings and drizzle the rest of the sauce over the top. Serve immediately.

Victoria sponges

MAKES

3 individual cakes

PREP AND COOK TIME

45 minutes

INGREDIENTS

300 g | 11 oz | 1 ½ cups butter

225 g | 8 oz | 1 cup caster (superfine) sugar

4 eggs

225 g | 8 oz | 2 cups self-raising flour

½ tsp vanilla extract

175 g | 6 oz | 2 cups icing (confectioners') sugar

160 g | 6 oz | ½ cup strawberry jam

icing (confectioners') sugar, to decorate

Heat the oven to 180°C (160° fan) 350F, gas 4. Grease and line six 7 ½ cm x 10 cm / 3 " x 4 " spring-sided cake tins with greaseproof paper.

Beat 225 g of the butter and the sugar in a mixing bowl until light and fluffy. Add the eggs, one at a time, beating well to combine. Add the flour and mix well.

Spoon the mixture into the tins and bake for 20-25 minutes until golden and springy to the touch. Allow the cakes to cool in the tins for 5 minutes, then place them on a wire rack to cool further.

Beat the remaining butter and vanilla extract until creamy. Sift in the icing sugar and beat until thick and smooth.

Spread the buttercream onto half of the cakes, then layer with jam. Finally place the remaining cakes on top and sandwich together. Dust generously with icing sugar.

Apple and blackberry pie

SERVES

4

PREP AND COOK TIME

2 hours

INGREDIENTS

225 g | 8 oz | 2 cups plain (all-purpose) flour

100 g | 3 ½ oz | ½ cup butter, chopped

30 g | 1 oz sugar

1 egg yolk

1-2 tbsp cream

For the filling:

150 ml | 5 fl. oz | ⅔ cup apple juice

200 ml | 7 fl. oz | ⅞ cup pear juice

30 g | 1 oz cornflour (corn starch)

75 g | 2 ½ oz | ⅓ cup sugar

200 g | 7 oz | 2 cups blackberries

4 cooking apples, peeled and diced

sugar, for sprinkling

200 ml | 7 fl. oz | ⅞ cup cream, whipped

For the pastry, rub the butter into the flour until the mixture resembles breadcrumbs. Add the rest of the pastry ingredients and work into a smooth dough, you may need to add a little water. Wrap the dough in cling film and chill for 30 minutes.

Heat oven to 200C (180C fan) 400F, gas 6 and butter a 1 ½ litre pie dish.

For the filling, put the apple juice and half of the pear juice into a pan and increase the heat to boiling point. Mix the rest of the pear juice with the cornflour and sugar and stir into the boiling liquid. Stir in the fruit, allow it to cool slightly and pour the filling into the pie dish.

Roll the pastry into a circle to fit the dish. Place on top of the filling, pressing the edges on firmly. Cut a small hole into the centre of the pie, or use a pie funnel to allow it to steam. Bake for about 40 minutes until the pastry is golden.

Sprinkle with sugar and serve with whipped cream.

Raspberry cheesecake

SERVES

8-10

PREP AND COOK TIME

1 hour 15 minutes

INGREDIENTS

150 g | 5 oz | 1 ½ cups digestive biscuits, crushed

50 g | 2 oz | ¼ cup unsalted butter, melted

110 g | 4 oz caster sugar

200 g | 7 oz | 1 cup cream cheese (soft cheese)

2 tbsp lemon juice

120 ml | 4 fl. oz | ½ cup cream

300 g | 11 oz | 2 ½ cups raspberries

100 g | 3 ½ oz | ½ cup sugar

30 ml | 1 fl. oz water

Grease a 20 cm / 8 " springform tin with butter. Stir the biscuit crumbs, melted butter and 2 tablespoons of sugar together. Press the mixture into the base of the tin and chill.

Beat the cream cheese with the remaining sugar and lemon juice. Whisk the cream until thick and stir into the cream cheese mixture, then spoon it over the biscuit base.

Cover with tin foil and freeze the cheesecake for 1 hour. Place in the refrigerator for 30 minutes before serving.

Heat the raspberries, water and sugar in a pan over a medium heat until the sugar has dissolved. Increase the heat to boiling point then simmer gently for a few minutes until the raspberries have softened. Pour into a sieve over a bowl and push the mixture through to make a purée.

Spoon the cooled purée over the cheesecake and serve.

Quince pudding

SERVES

4-6

PREP AND COOK TIME

55 minutes

INGREDIENTS

1 kg | 2 lbs ripe quinces

200 ml | 7 fl. oz | 1 cup port wine

1 cinnamon stick

200 g | 7 oz | 2 cups plain (all-purpose) flour

a pinch of salt

3 tsp baking powder

150 g | 5 oz | 1 cup butter

150 ml | 5 fl. oz | 1 cup buttermilk

80 g | 3 oz | ½ cup sugar

Heat the port wine in a pan with the cinnamon stick and increase the heat to boiling point. Add the quince slices and remove from the heat. Cover and leave it to cool for 15 minutes.

Heat the oven to 200°C (180° fan) 400F, gas 6. Grease a pie dish or baking dish with butter.

Remove the cinnamon stick from the quinces. Place the quince slices and the liquid in the baking dish.

Sift the flour, salt and baking powder into a mixing bowl and rub in the butter until the mixture resembles breadcrumbs. Stir in the buttermilk and sugar and mix to form a soft dough.

Place the dough on top of the quince slices and bake for 25-30 minutes until golden brown.

Raspberry tiramisu

SERVES

6-8

PREP AND COOK TIME

3 hours 25 minutes

INGREDIENTS

30 sponge fingers

300 ml | 11 fl. oz | 1 ⅓ cups espresso

1 small lemon, zest and juice

500 g | 1 lb | 2 ¼ cups mascarpone

45 g | 1 ½ oz sugar

250 g | 9 oz | 2 cups raspberries

100 g | 3 ½ oz dark (plain) chocolate, grated

1 tbsp cocoa powder

Line the base of a large baking dish with half the sponge fingers. Sprinkle with half the espresso.

Mix the lemon zest and juice with the mascarpone and sugar. Carefully spread half of the mascarpone on the sponge fingers in the dish. Scatter half of the raspberries over the mascarpone and press in.

Sprinkle a generous amount of the grated chocolate over the raspberry and mascarpone layer. Place another layer of sponge fingers on top and sprinkle with the rest of the espresso. Spread the remaining mascarpone on top.

Sprinkle with more chocolate. Place the remaining raspberries on top and scatter with the remaining chocolate then sift the cocoa to dust. Chill for at least 3 hours before serving.

Apple crumble

SERVES

4

PREP AND COOK TIME

45 minutes

INGREDIENTS

4-5 cooking apples, peeled and sliced

60 g | 2 oz brown sugar

1 tbsp lemon juice

50 ml | 2 fl. oz white wine

100 g | 3 ½ oz | ¾ cup chopped walnuts

1 tsp cinnamon

50 g | 2 oz | ⅓ cup raisins

100 g | 3 ½ oz | ½ cup butter

175 g | 6 oz | 1 ½ cups self-raising flour

100 g | 3 ½ oz | ½ cup sugar

Heat the oven to 200°C (180° fan) 400F, gas 6 and grease a baking dish with butter.

Mix together the apples, sugar, lemon juice, white wine, half the walnuts, cinnamon and raisins and pour into the baking dish.

Rub the butter and flour together until the mixture resembles breadcrumbs. Sprinkle evenly over the apple and scatter with the remaining walnuts.

Bake for 30 minutes until the apples are tender and the crumble is browned. Serve warm with custard or ice-cream.

Lemon meringue pie

SERVES

4-6

PREP AND COOK TIME

1 hour 30 minutes

INGREDIENTS

225 g | 8 oz shortcrust pie pastry

For the filling:

200 g | 7 oz | 1 cup caster
(superfine) sugar

2 lemons, zest and juice

1 egg yolk, beaten

1 tbsp cornflour, mixed with a little milk

175 ml | 6 fl. oz | ¾ cup boiling water

2 egg whites

a pinch of salt

75 g | 2 ½ oz | ⅓ cup caster sugar

Heat the oven to 200°C (180° fan) 400F, gas 6 and grease a 20 cm / 8 " flan tin.

Roll out the pastry on a floured surface and line the tin with it. Prick the base with a fork, then place a circle of greaseproof paper over the base of the pastry and cover with ceramic baking beans (or uncooked rice).

Blind bake the pastry case for 18-20 minutes until lightly golden. Remove from the oven and remove the baking beans or rice and the greaseproof paper.

Reduce the oven temperature 150°C (130° fan) 300F, gas 2.

For the filling, put the sugar, the lemon zest and juice into a saucepan. Mix the egg yolk with the cornflour mixture, then add to the pan with the boiling water. Increase the heat to boiling point whilst stirring, then simmer over a low heat, stirring constantly, until it has thickened. Remove from the heat and allow it to cool. Pour the cooled filling into the pastry case.

For the meringue topping, whisk the egg whites until stiff peaks form. Whisk in a tablespoon of sugar, then add the remaining sugar, a tablespoon at a time.

Spread the meringue topping over the pie filling and bake for 45-50 minutes, until the meringue is lightly golden and crisp on the outside, but soft underneath.

Plum pies

SERVES

6

PREP AND COOK TIME

45 minutes

INGREDIENTS

200 g | 7 oz | 2 cups plain (all-purpose) flour

3 ½ tbsp butter

50 g | 2 oz | ½ cup sugar

12 egg yolks, beaten

a pinch of salt

250 g | 9 oz | 1 ½ cups cream (soft) cheese

30 g | 1 oz sugar

30 g | 1 oz semolina

1 tbsp lemon juice

1 tsp vanilla extract

12 plums, pitted and halved

50 g | 2 oz | 1 cup flaked almonds

icing (confectioners') sugar

Mix the flour, salt and sugar together in a mixing bowl. Rub in the butter until the mixture resembles breadcrumbs, and then stir in half of the egg yolk to form a soft dough. Wrap the dough in cling film and chill for 20 minutes.

Heat the oven to 200°C (180° fan) 400F, gas 6. Grease six small baking dishes with butter, each roughly 10 cm / 4 " in diameter.

Mix the cream cheese with the sugar, semolina, lemon juice and vanilla. Roll the dough out on a floured surface into a large square and cut out 6 squares. Place the squares in the baking dishes.

Spoon the cream cheese mixture in to the baking dishes and cover with plum halves. Brush with the remaining egg yolk, sprinkle with almonds and a little icing sugar. Bake for 30 minutes until golden brown. Remove from the dishes and allow them to cool on a wire rack.

Serve with whipped cream or ice-cream.

Pumpkin pie

SERVES

4-6

PREP AND COOK TIME

1 hour

INGREDIENTS

225 g | 8 oz shortcrust (pie) pastry

225 g | 8 oz | 1 cup fresh pumpkin puree, or

canned pumpkin

2 eggs, beaten

150 ml | 5 fl. oz | 1 cup cream

75 g | 2 ½ oz | ½ cup dark brown sugar

1 tsp ground cinnamon

½ tsp ground ginger

a pinch of ground cloves

a pinch of grated nutmeg

½ tsp mixed spice

Heat the oven to 190°C (170° fan) 375F, gas 5. Grease a 23 cm / 9 " flan tin.

Roll out the pastry and line the tin. Place the remaining ingredients in a mixing bowl and beat well until combined.

Pour the mixture into the pastry case and bake for 40-50 minutes until the filling has set. Leave to cool in the tin. Serve warm with whipped cream.

Ginger puddings

SERVES

4

PREP AND COOK TIME

55 minutes

INGREDIENTS

60 g | 2 oz | ½ cup butter, melted

175 g | 6 oz | 1 cup caster (superfine) sugar

1 egg

175 g | 6 oz | 1 ½ cups plain (all-purpose) flour

1 tsp ground ginger

2 tbsp stem (candied) ginger, finely chopped

½ tsp vanilla extract

50 ml | 2 fl. oz milk

125 g | 4 ½ oz | ½ cup butter

375 g | 13 oz | 2 cups light brown sugar

500 ml | 18 fl. oz | 2 cups cream

Heat the oven to 170°C (150° fan) 325F, gas 3. Grease 4 small pudding moulds with butter.

Whisk the butter, sugar and egg together in a mixing bowl. Gradually fold in the flour, ground and stem ginger and vanilla extract until blended. Add the milk to give a soft dropping consistency, adding a bit more if needed.

Spoon the mixture into the moulds and bake for 35 minutes. Test with a wooden toothpick, if it comes out clean, the puddings are cooked.

Melt the butter in a pan. Stir in the sugar, and then add the cream. Increase the heat to boiling point, and cook for 3 minutes, continuously stirring.

Turn the moulds upside down and tap them out onto serving plates. Pour over the sticky toffee sauce. Serve immediately with custard.

Pecan and treacle tart

SERVES
4-6

PREP AND COOK TIME
1 hour 45 minutes

225 g | 8 oz | 2 cups plain (all-purpose) flour

a pinch of salt

30 g | 1 oz caster (superfine) sugar

155 g | 5 ½ oz | ⅔ cup unsalted butter

1 egg yolk, mixed with 1 tbsp water

For the filling:

300 g | 11 oz | 1 ½ cups dark brown sugar

230 g | 8 oz | 1 cup unsalted butter

170 ml | 6 fl. oz | ¾ cup black treacle (molasses)

170 ml | 6 fl. oz | ¾ cup golden (corn) syrup

5 eggs, beaten

1 tsp vanilla extract

300 g | 11 oz | 2 cups coarsely chopped
pecan nuts

110 g | 4 oz | 1 cup pine nuts

8-10 whole pecan nuts

50 g | 2 oz | ½ cup pine nuts, toasted

icing (confectioners') sugar

Heat the oven to 200°C (180° fan) 400F, gas 6 and grease a 25 cm / 10 " springform tin with butter.

For the pastry, sift the flour, salt and sugar into a mixing bowl. Rub in the butter until the mixture resembles fine crumbs. Stir in the egg yolk and water and mix together to form a soft dough. Wrap the dough in cling film and chill for 15 minutes.

Roll out the dough on a floured surface to a circle about 33 cm / 13 " in diameter and line the tin. Prick the bottom of the pastry case with a fork, then chill for 10 minutes.

Bake the pastry case for about 20 minutes, until very lightly brown and then leave to cool.

Reduce the oven temperature to 150°C (130° fan) 300°F, gas 2.

Heat the sugar, butter, treacle and golden syrup in a large saucepan and increase the heat to boiling point. Simmer gently for 5 minutes, stirring frequently to prevent sticking, then remove from the heat.

Mix the eggs with the vanilla extract, chopped pecans and pine nuts until well blended. Stir in the syrup mixture and mix until smooth.

Pour the filling into the baked pastry case and place the whole pecans on top, pressing them into the filling. Bake for 1 hour until the filling is just firm to the touch.

To decorate, scatter over the pine nuts and sift over a little icing sugar.

Bread pudding

SERVES

4-6

PREP AND COOK TIME

35 minutes

INGREDIENTS

1 stick rhubarb

50 ml | 2 fl. oz dry white wine

30 g | 1 oz sugar

6 slices white bread

200 ml | 7 fl. oz | 1 cup cream

4 eggs

seeds from a vanilla pod (bean)

½ tsp cinnamon

icing (confectioners') sugar

Heat the oven to 200°C (180° fan) 400F, gas 6. Grease a baking dish with a bit of butter.

Cut the rhubarb into thin strips. Put the white wine in to a pan and heat it to boiling point. Add the rhubarb and half the sugar and leave to simmer for 10 minutes until the rhubarb is tender.

Arrange the bread neatly in the baking dish, overlapping the slices. Whisk the cream with the eggs, vanilla seeds, cinnamon and the remaining sugar and pour over the bread.

Place the cooked rhubarb over the top and bake for 20 minutes, until golden brown. Dust with icing sugar before serving.

Chocolate and nut meringue

SERVES
4-6

PREP AND COOK TIME
1 hour 10 minutes

INGREDIENTS
6 egg whites

350 g | 12 oz | 1 ½ cups caster (superfine) sugar

300 ml | 11 fl. oz | 1 ½ cups double cream

1 tbsp icing (confectioners') sugar

1 tbsp cocoa

30 ml | 1 fl. oz hazelnut liqueur

400 g | 14 oz chocolate hazelnut spread

To decorate:

75 g | 2 ½ oz plain chocolate, grated

75 g | 2 ½ oz | ½ cup chopped, roasted hazelnuts

Heat the oven to 190°C (170° fan) 375F, gas 5. Line 3 baking trays with greaseproof paper.

Whisk the egg whites in a bowl until stiff peaks form. Whisk in the sugar, a spoonful at a time until shiny and stiff, then whisk in the vinegar.

Divide the meringue into 3 equal portions. Spread a round shape for each portion on each baking tray. Bake for 35-40 minutes until crisp.

Turn the oven off and allow the meringues to cool. When the meringues are cold, peel away the baking paper.

Whisk the cream until thick. Sift in the icing sugar, cocoa and liqueur and whisk until it is softly peaking.

Place a meringue on a serving plate and carefully spread with the hazelnut cream. Place the second meringue on top.

Beat the chocolate hazelnut spread to soften and then carefully spread it on the second meringue.

Place the final meringue disc on top and scatter with the grated chocolate and hazelnuts. Serve immediately.

Chocolate puddings

SERVES

4

PREP AND COOK TIME

40 minutes

INGREDIENTS

125 g | 4 ½ oz plain chocolate, chopped

125 g | 4 ½ oz | ½ cup butter

2 eggs

3 egg yolks

60 g | 2 oz | ½ cup sugar

a pinch of salt

25 g | 1 oz flour

To serve:

whipped cream

Heat the oven to 180°C (160° fan) 350F, gas 4. Brush 6 ramekins with melted butter and chill.

Melt the chocolate and butter in a heatproof bowl over a pan of simmering water. Whisk the eggs, egg yolks, sugar and salt for 8-10 minutes until very creamy.

Gradually stir in the chocolate mixture. Sift in the flour and gently stir together. Spoon the mixture into the ramekins and bake for 15 minutes. The centre of the puddings will still have a liquid consistency.

Carefully remove the puddings from the ramekins and place on serving plates. Serve with cream.

Pavlova

SERVES

4-6

PREP AND COOK TIME

2 hours 20 minutes

INGREDIENTS

6 egg whites

350 g | 12 oz | 1 ½ cups caster (superfine) sugar

30 g | 1 oz cornflour (cornstarch)

2 tsp white vinegar

1 tsp vanilla extract

300 ml | 11 fl. oz | 1 ½ cups cream

675 g | 1 ½ lbs | 1 ½ cups mixed berries

mint leaves

icing (confectioners') sugar, to decorate

Heat the oven to 200°C (180° fan) 400F, gas 6. Line 2 baking trays with non-stick baking paper.

Whisk the egg whites with an electric whisk on a high speed until stiff. Gradually whisk in the sugar and continue to whisk at low speed until the sugar is fully combined. Whisk in the cornflour, vinegar and vanilla extract.

Using a large spoon, palette knife or piping bag, place half of the meringue mixture onto a baking tray in the shape of a large circle. Repeat with the remaining meringue mixture on the second baking tray.

Place the baking trays in the oven and immediately reduce the oven temperature to the lowest setting. Bake for 1-2 hours until dry, firm and crisp.

Remove the meringues from the oven and allow to cool. Carefully remove the paper and place a meringue on a serving plate.

Whisk the cream until thick and carefully spread over the meringue. Place most of the berries on top of the cream. Place the other meringue on top to sandwich together.

Decorate the top with the remaining berries, mint leaves and a sprinkling of icing sugar.

Baking bread

Pumpkin bread

MAKES

1 loaf

PREP AND COOK TIME

2 hours 25 minutes

INGREDIENTS

42 g | 1 ½ oz fresh yeast

250 ml | 9 fl. oz | 1 cup warm water

1 tsp sugar

400 g | 14 oz | 3 ½ cups strong

wholemeal flour

250 g | 9 oz | 5 cups grated pumpkin flesh

100 g | 3 ½ oz | 1 cup ground hazelnuts

1 tsp salt

1 egg, beaten

Crumble the yeast into 50 ml of warm water in a small bowl and stir in the sugar. Leave to stand for 10 minutes until frothy.

Mix the flour, pumpkin, hazelnuts and salt together in a mixing bowl. Pour in the yeast mixture, remaining warm water and the egg and then mix with your hands into a dough. If the dough is too stiff, add 1-2 tablespoons of warm water; if it is too soft, add a little more flour.

Cover the bowl with a tea towel or cling film and leave in a warm place for 45 minutes, until doubled in size.

Punch down the dough and turn it out onto a floured surface. Knead for a few minutes, then place it into a greased loaf tin. Cover as before and leave in a warm place to rise for 45 minutes.

Heat the oven to 200°C (180° fan) 400F, gas 6. Bake for 1 hour until browned on top. Test with a wooden toothpick, if it comes out clean, the bread is done.

Allow the loaf to cool in the tin for 5 minutes, then remove it and place onto a wire rack to cool completely.

Classic round white

MAKES

1 loaf

PREP AND COOK TIME

3 hours

INGREDIENTS

500 g | 1 lb | 4 cups strong white bread flour

2 ½ tbsp butter

2 sachets yeast

2 tsp salt

300 ml | 11 fl. oz | 1 ½ cups warm water

sunflower oil

Put the flour into a mixing bowl and add the butter. Add the yeast and salt and stir.

Add half the water and mix with your fingers. Continue to add water a little at a time, until the mixture forms a soft dough.

Lightly grease a work surface with a little oil and turn out the dough. Knead for 10 minutes until the dough is smooth and elastic.

Lightly grease the mixing bowl with a little oil and put the dough back into it. Cover with a tea towel or lightly oiled cling film and place the bowl in a warm place for 1-2 hours, until the dough has doubled in size.

Place the dough onto a lightly floured surface and knead it firmly to 'knock out' the air. Shape the dough into a round loaf shape.

Line a baking tray with greaseproof paper. Place the dough on the baking tray, cover with a tea towel or lightly oiled cling film and leave in a warm place for 1 hour, until doubled in size.

Heat the oven to 220°C (200° fan) 425F, gas 7.

Sprinkle some flour on top of the dough and very gently rub it in. Use a large, sharp knife to make shallow cuts in the dough, about 1 cm / ½ " deep.

Bake for 30 minutes until risen and golden. Remove from the baking tray and place onto a wire rack to cool.

Banana bread

MAKES

1 loaf

PREP AND COOK TIME

1 hour 15 minutes

INGREDIENTS

175 g | 6 oz | 1 ½ cups plain (all-purpose) flour

50 g | 2 oz | ½ cup wholemeal flour

2 tsp baking powder

½ tsp grated nutmeg

1 tsp ground cinnamon

2 eggs, beaten

110 g | 4 oz | ½ cup butter

225 g | 8 oz | 1 ½ cups brown sugar

1 tsp vanilla extract

a pinch of salt

50 g | 2 oz | ½ cup sultanas

60 g | 2 oz chopped pecan nuts

6 bananas, mashed

Heat the oven to 180°C (160° fan) 350F, gas 4. Grease a loaf tin with butter.

Beat the butter and sugar together in a mixing bowl until light and fluffy. Add the vanilla extract and eggs, beating the mixture thoroughly. Mix the dry ingredients together and stir into the egg mixture. Add the sultanas, pecan nuts and mashed bananas and mix thoroughly.

Spoon into the loaf tin and bake for 1 hour. Test with a wooden toothpick, if it comes out clean, the loaf is cooked. Remove from the oven and allow to cool in the tin for 10 minutes, and then place on a wire rack to cool completely.

Crusty rye bread

MAKES

1 loaf

PREP AND COOK TIME

40 minutes

INGREDIENTS

500 g | 1 lb | 4 cups rye flour

500 g | 1 lb | 4 cups strong white bread flour

½ sachet yeast

20 g | 1 oz salt

700 ml | 25 fl. oz | 3 cups warm water

Put the dry ingredients in a large mixing bowl and stir to combine. Pour in the water and mix well with your hands to form a dough.

Place the dough onto a floured surface and knead for 10 minutes until smooth and elastic. Grease a large baking tray. Shape the dough into a long oval and coat with a little more flour.

Cover with a tea towel or cling film and leave in a warm place to rise for 1-2 hours, until doubled in size.

Heat the oven to 220°C (200° fan) 425F, gas 7.

Sprinkle some flour on top of the dough and very gently rub it in. Using a large, sharp knife, make shallow cuts about 1 cm / ½ " deep. Bake for 10 minutes, then reduce the oven temperature to 180°C (160° fan) 350F, gas 4 and cook for a further 25-30 minutes. Remove the loaf from the oven and cool on a wire rack.

Polenta bread

MAKES

1 loaf

PREP AND COOK TIME

40 minutes

INGREDIENTS

3 ½ tbsp butter, melted

500 ml | 18 fl. oz | 2 cups milk

2 large eggs

320 g | 11 oz | 2 cups polenta (cornmeal)

60 g | 2 oz | ½ cup cornflour (cornstarch)

6 tsp baking powder

3 tsp sugar

1 tsp salt

To serve:

Tomato relish

Heat the oven to 200°C (180° fan) 400F, gas 6. Grease a rectangular baking dish.

Whisk together the butter, milk and eggs in a mixing bowl. In a separate bowl, mix together the polenta, cornflour, baking powder, sugar and salt. Stir into the egg mixture.

Spoon into the baking dish and bake for 20-30 minutes until golden. Test with a wooden toothpick, if it comes out clean, the bread is cooked. Serve warm with tomato relish.

Walnut loaf

MAKES

1 loaf

PREP AND COOK TIME

1 hour

INGREDIENTS

200 g | 7 oz | 2 cups chopped walnuts

350 g | 12 oz | 3 ½ cups strong
white bread flour

350 g | 12 oz | 3 ½ cups strong
wholemeal bread flour

1 tsp salt

1 sachet yeast

400 ml | 14 fl. oz | 2 cups warm water

30 ml | 1 fl. oz walnut oil

1 tbsp clear honey

Heat the oven to 200°C (180° fan) 400F, gas 6. Grease a baking tray with a little oil.

Put the walnuts on the baking tray and toast them in the oven for 8-10 minutes until lightly browned. Remove from the oven and set them aside to cool.

Put both flours, salt and yeast in a mixing bowl and stir. Mix the water, walnut oil and honey together and stir into the flour mixture with the toasted walnuts. Mix with your hands to a soft dough. If the dough is too stiff, add more warm water.

Turn the dough out onto a lightly floured work surface and knead for 10 minutes. Shape the dough into a neat oval shape and place onto the baking tray. Cover with a tea towel or cling film and leave in a warm place to rise for an hour, until doubled in size. Bake for 35 minutes until golden brown. Remove from the tin and allow the loaf to cool on a wire rack.

Rosemary and garlic focaccia

MAKES

2 focaccias

PREP AND COOK TIME

1 hour 45 minutes

INGREDIENTS

21 g | 1 oz fresh yeast

200 ml | 7 fl. oz | 1 cup warm water

400 g | 14 oz | 4 cups strong white bread flour

½ tsp salt

50 ml | 2 fl. oz | 10 tsp olive oil

2 shallots, chopped

30 g | 1 oz fresh rosemary, chopped

30 g | 1 fl. oz olive oil

coarse sea salt

Crumble the yeast into the water. Mix the flour with the salt in a mixing bowl. Stir in the dissolved yeast with the olive oil and mix to a dough. Cover with a tea towel or cling film and leave in a warm place to rise for 45 minutes, until it has doubled in size.

Place the dough onto a floured surface and knead well until smooth and elastic. Knead in 1 shallot and 1 tablespoon of rosemary.

Grease 2 baking trays. Divide the dough in 2 pieces, each 16 cm x 20 cm / 6 " x 8 " in diameter. Place on the baking trays. Press into the surface with the knuckles to make small impressions in the dough. Prick the dough several times with a fork.

Brush with olive oil and sprinkle with some coarse sea salt and the remaining shallots and rosemary. Cover and leave in a warm place to rise for 15 minutes.

Heat the oven to 200°C (180° fan) 400F, gas 6.

Bake the focaccias for 25 minutes until golden and cooked through.

Chocolate plait

MAKES

1 loaf

PREP AND COOK TIME

3 hours 30 minutes

INGREDIENTS

350 g | 12 oz | 3 ½ cups white bread flour

30 g | 1 oz | ½ cup cocoa powder

7 g | 1/4 oz yeast

150 ml | 5 fl. oz | 1 cup milk

110 g | 4 oz | ½ cup sugar

50 g | 2 oz | ½ cup butter

1 egg

75 g | 2 ½ oz | ½ cup chopped pecans

30 g | 1 oz | ½ cup pitted dates, chopped

1 tbsp grated orange zest

75 g | 2 ½ oz | ½ cup plain

chocolate chips, melted

Stir 100 g of the flour, all of the cocoa powder and yeast together in a mixing bowl. Heat the milk, sugar, butter and salt in a pan until the butter has almost melted.

Add the two mixtures together and the egg. Beat with an electric whisk for 30 seconds, scraping the side of the bowl constantly. Beat for a further 3 minutes. Using a wooden spoon, stir in the pecans, chopped dates and orange zest. Stir in some of the remaining flour to form a very soft dough.

Turn the dough out onto a lightly floured surface. Lightly grease the mixing bowl. Add the rest of the flour and knead to make a moderately soft dough that is smooth and elastic. Shape the dough into a ball. Place in the lightly greased bowl. Cover the dough with a tea towel or cling film and leave it to rise in a warm place for 1 hour until it has doubled in size.

Punch the dough down in the bowl. Place the dough onto a lightly floured surface. Divide the dough into three pieces. Cover and leave for 10 minutes. Lightly grease a baking tray. Shape each portion of dough into a 43 cm / 16 " long strip. Place the strips 2 ½ cm / 1 " apart on the baking tray. Braid the strips together and press the ends together to seal and tuck underneath. Cover and leave to rise in a warm place, for an hour to rise until doubled in size. Heat the oven to 160°C (140° fan) 325F, gas 3. Bake for 35 minutes. If necessary, cover loosely with foil for the last 10 minutes of baking to prevent over-browning.

Soda bread

SERVES
1 loaf

PREP AND COOK TIME
50 minutes

INGREDIENTS
350 g | 12 oz | 3 cups wholemeal flour

125 g | 4 ½ oz | 1 cup coarse oatmeal

2 tsp bicarbonate of soda (baking soda)

1 tsp salt

1 tsp liquid honey

300 ml | 11 fl. oz | 1 ½ cups buttermilk

45 ml | 1 ½ fl. oz milk

Heat the oven to 200°C (180° fan) 400F, gas 6. Grease a baking tray with a little oil.

Mix the flour with the oatmeal, bicarbonate of soda and salt in a mixing bowl. Stir in the honey, buttermilk and enough milk to make a soft dough.

Knead lightly for 5 minutes until smooth. Shape the dough into a 20 cm / 8 " round and place on the baking tray.

Cut a deep cross into the centre of the dough. Brush with a little milk and bake for 30-35 minutes until the bread is risen and firm.

Cinnamon rolls

MAKES

8 rolls

PREP AND COOK TIME

1 hour 45 minutes

INGREDIENTS

225 g | 8 oz | 2 cups strong white bread flour

50 g | 2 oz | ½ cup caster (superfine) sugar

a pinch of salt

25 g | 1 oz | butter

7 g | ¼ oz yeast

1 egg, beaten

125 ml | 4 ½ fl. oz | ½ cup warm milk

1 tbsp ground cinnamon

85 g | 3 oz | ½ cup light brown sugar

100 g | 3 ½ oz | 1 cup chopped pecans

50 g | 2 oz | ½ cup butter, melted

60 ml | 2 fl. oz maple syrup

50 g | 2 oz | ½ cup pecan nuts, chopped

Put the flour, sugar and salt in a mixing bowl, then rub in the butter until the mixture resembles breadcrumbs.

Stir in the yeast, egg and milk and mix well until the mixture forms a soft dough. Turn onto a lightly floured surface and knead for 10 minutes until smooth and elastic. Lightly oil the mixing bowl.

Put the dough into the greased bowl and cover with a tea towel or cling film and leave it to rise in a warm place for 1 hour or until it has doubled in size. Combine the cinnamon, sugar and pecans in a food processor, then blend until the nuts are finely ground.

Punch down the dough and knead to remove the air. Roll and stretch the dough on a floured surface to form a 23 cm x 30 cm / 9 " x 12 " rectangle. Brush the dough with half of the melted butter and sprinkle over the sugar, cinnamon and pecans.

Roll up the dough tightly, like a swiss roll, starting at the longer edge. Press the edges to seal, then cut it into 8 slices. Grease 2 baking trays with butter. Put the buns on the trays, cover and leave in a warm place for 30 minutes, until they have doubled in size.

Heat the oven to 190°C (170° fan) 375F, gas 5. Bake the buns for 30 minutes until golden. Remove from the oven and place on a wire rack to cool.

Heat the maple syrup, sugar and remaining melted butter in a pan, stirring. Drizzle the maple syrup glaze over the buns and sprinkle the pecans on top of them.

Wholemeal loaf

MAKES

1 loaf

PREP AND COOK TIME

1 hour 45 minutes

INGREDIENTS

500 g | 1 lb | 4 ½ cups granary bread flour

7 g | ¼ oz yeast

1 tsp salt

300 ml | 11 fl. oz | 1 ½ cups warm water

30 ml | 1 fl. oz sunflower oil

1 tbsp sugar

Grease a loaf tin with butter.

Mix the flour, yeast and salt in a mixing bowl. Stir in the water with the oil and sugar, to form a soft dough. Place the dough onto a lightly floured surface and knead for 5 minutes until smooth.

Put the dough in the loaf tin, pressing it in evenly. Cover with a tea towel or cling film and leave in a warm place to rise, for 1 hour, until the dough has risen to fill the tin.

Heat the oven to 200°C (180° fan) 400F, gas 6.

Make several slashes across the top of the loaf with a sharp knife, and then bake for 30-35 minutes, until the loaf is risen and golden. Remove from the tin and place the loaf onto a wire rack to cool.

Apple and cinnamon loaf

MAKES

1 loaf

PREP AND COOK TIME

1 hour

INGREDIENTS

250 g | 9 oz | 2 ½ cups plain (all-purpose) flour

a pinch of salt

1 tsp baking powder

225 g | 8 oz | 1 cup sugar

2 tsp ground cinnamon

110 g | 4 oz | ½ cup butter, melted

1 egg

110 ml | 4 fl. oz milk

175 g | 6 oz | 1 ½ cups apples, diced

50 g | 2 oz | ½ cup raisins

2 tbsp demerara sugar

Heat the oven to 180°C (160° fan) 350F, gas 4. Lightly grease a loaf tin with butter.

Mix the flour, salt, baking powder, sugar and cinnamon together in a bowl. Mix the melted butter, egg and milk together in a separate bowl. Gently stir in the apples and raisins.

Stir into the flour mixture until well blended. Spoon the mixture into the loaf tin and sprinkle the top with 1 tablespoon of demerara sugar.

Bake for 35-45 minutes until golden and cooked through. Sprinkle the remaining demerara sugar over the hot loaf. Remove from the oven and allow it to cool in the tin for 10 minutes, then place the loaf on a wire rack to cool completely.

Goat's cheese and olive loaf

MAKES

1 loaf

PREP AND COOK TIME

1 hour

INGREDIENTS

150 ml | 5 fl. oz water

4 eggs

250 g | 9 oz self-raising flour

60 g | 2oz sundried tomatoes

110 g | 4oz black olives, pitted, halved

2 sprigs rosemary, chopped

110 g | 4 oz goat's cheese, sliced

To garnish:

rosemary sprigs

Heat the oven to 200°C (180° fan) 400F, gas 6. Grease a loaf tins with butter.

Knead the rosemary, sundried tomatoes and most of the olives into the dough. Beat the water and eggs until frothy. Sift in the flour and mix until smooth. Gently combine half of the cheese into the dough. Put the dough into the loaf tin. Press the remaining olives into the top of the dough.

Bake for 15 minutes, then place the remaining cheese slices on top of the loaf and cook for a further 15 minutes until golden.

Cool in the tins for 10 minutes, then remove and garnish with rosemary sprigs.

Hot cross buns

MAKES

12 buns

PREP AND COOK TIME

2 hours

INGREDIENTS

For the buns:

675 g | 1 ½ lb | 6 cups strong white bread flour

1 tsp salt

75 g | 2 ½ oz | ½ cup butter

1 tsp ground cinnamon

1 tsp ground mixed spice

a pinch of nutmeg

50 g | 2 oz | ½ cup light brown sugar

200 g | 7 oz | 1 cup mixed dried fruit

25 g | 1 oz | 1 cup candied peel, chopped

7 oz | ¼ oz yeast

325 ml | 11 fl. oz | 1 ½ cups warm milk

2 eggs

75 g | 2 ½ oz | ¾ cup plain (all-purpose) flour

60 ml | 2 fl. oz milk

30 g | 1 oz caster (superfine) sugar

Sift the bread flour and salt into a mixing bowl. Rub in the butter until the mixture resembles breadcrumbs. Stir in the spices, sugar, dried fruit, candied peel and yeast.

Make a well in the centre. Beat the milk and eggs together and pour into the bread flour mixture. Mix well to a soft dough. Place onto a floured surface and knead for 10 minutes until smooth and elastic. Place in an oiled bowl, cover with a tea towel or cling film and leave to rise in a warm place for 45 minutes.

Place the dough onto a floured surface and knead again lightly for a few minutes to knock out any air bubbles. Divide into 12 pieces and shape into buns.

Grease a baking tray. Place the buns well apart on the tray, cover loosely with cling film and leave to rise in a warm place for 45 minutes, until doubled in size. Mark a cross in the top of each bun with a sharp knife.

Heat the oven to 200°C (180° fan) 400F, gas 6.

Mix the flour for the crosses with enough water to form a very loose paste. Spoon the mixture into a piping bag and pipe a cross onto each bun.

Bake for 15-20 minutes until golden. Heat the milk and sugar in a small pan and simmer for 2 minutes. Remove the buns from the oven and brush with the glaze while still warm. Remove from the baking tray and allow them to cool on a wire rack.

Rustic sourdough

MAKES
1 loaf

PREP AND COOK TIME
45 minutes
(extra time needed
for starter and rising)

INGREDIENTS

For the sourdough starter:
410 g | 15 oz | 3 ½ cups strong
white bread flour
100 ml | 3 ½ fl. oz lukewarm water

For the dough:
500 g | 1 lb | 4 ½ cups strong
white bread flour
1 tsp salt
240 ml | 8 fl. oz | 1 cup lukewarm water

For the sourdough starter, stir 110 g of the flour and the water together in a bowl to make a sticky paste. Cover with a damp tea towel and leave at room temperature for 2 days, keeping the tea towel moistened. After 2 days the mixture should be bubbly and have a milky odour. If it looks mouldy or smells sour or bad, throw it away and start again.

To feed the starter, stir in another 100 g of flour and enough lukewarm water to make a soft dough. Cover the bowl and leave at room temperature for 24 hours. It should look very bubbly. Stir well and then discard half of the starter. Add another 100 g flour and enough lukewarm water to make a dough, as before. Cover again and leave for 12 hours. It should now be very bubbly.

For the dough, mix the flour with the salt in a mixing bowl and make a well in the centre. Weigh out 200 g of the sourdough starter and mix it with the water, then pour it into the well in the flour. Gradually work the flour into the liquid mixture to make a soft dough. Turn out the dough onto a floured surface and knead for about 10 minutes or until very pliable. Return it to the cleaned mixing bowl, cover with a damp tea towel and leave in a warm place to rise until doubled in size, about 3-6 hours.

Turn out the risen dough onto a floured surface and knock it back. Shape the dough into a ball and place in a bowl. Heat the oven to 220°C (200° fan) 425F, gas 7 and lightly grease a large baking tray with oil. Place the dough on the baking tray and slash the top with a sharp knife. Bake for about 35 minutes or until golden brown.

Banana loaf

MAKES

1 loaf

PREP AND COOK TIME

1 hour

INGREDIENTS

125 g | 4 ½ oz | ½ cup butter

125 g | 4 ½ oz | 1 cup sugar

3 eggs, separated

a pinch of salt

200 g | 7 oz | 2 cups plain (all-purpose) flour

1 tsp baking powder

50 g | 2 oz | ½ cup ground hazelnuts

3 small bananas

30 ml | 1 fl. oz lemon juice

Heat the oven to 180°C (160° fan) 350F, gas 4. Grease a loaf tin with butter.

Beat the butter and sugar in a mixing bowl until fluffy. Gradually beat in the egg yolks until smooth. Whisk the egg whites with the salt in a separate bowl until stiff.

Sift the flour and baking powder into the egg whites and gently stir in the ground hazelnuts. Mash the bananas with the lemon juice and fold into the egg yolk mixture. Gradually add the egg white mixture until thoroughly blended.

Spoon the mixture into the loaf tin and bake for 45 minutes until golden. Remove from the oven and allow to cool in the tin for 10 minutes. Remove the loaf from the tin and place onto a wire rack to cool completely.

Rustic rye bread

MAKES

1 loaf

PREP AND COOK TIME

3 hour

(extra time needed for rising)

INGREDIENTS

500 g | 1 lb | 4 ½ cups dark rye flour

30 g | 1 oz fresh yeast

430 ml | 15 fl. oz | 2 cups water

40 ml | 1 ½ fl. oz black treacle (molasses)

2 tsp salt

Put half of the rye flour in a bowl and add half of the yeast and 200 ml of the water. Mix together very well then cover with a tea towel or cling film and leave to rise for 9 hours or overnight.

Line a baking tray with greaseproof paper. Add the remaining ingredients to the dough and knead well for 5 minutes.

Shape the dough into a ball and place it on a baking tray. Cover with a tea towel or cling film and leave in a warm place to rise for 2 hours, until doubled in size.

Heat the oven to 220°C (200° fan) 425F, gas 7. Bake the loaf for 40 minutes until cooked through. Remove the loaf from the tray and place it on a wire rack to cool.

Bacon cornbread

MAKES
1 loaf

PREP AND COOK TIME
55 minutes

INGREDIENTS
1 tsp oil

350 g | 12 oz smoked, streaky bacon, finely chopped

2 spring onions (scallions), finely chopped

120 g | 4 oz | ½ cup sweetcorn

½ tsp chilli flakes

350 g | 12 oz | 2 cups cornmeal

350 g | 12 oz | 3 cups gluten-free white flour

1 tsp sugar

1 tsp gluten-free baking powder

½ tsp bicarbonate of soda (baking soda)

½ tsp salt

375 ml | 13 fl. oz | 1 ½ cups buttermilk

2 eggs

2 tsp melted butter

1 tsp maple syrup

½ tsp freshly ground black pepper

Grease a loaf tin with butter. Heat the oven to 200°C (180° fan) 400F, gas 6.

Heat the oil in a frying pan and fry the bacon for 2 minutes. Add the spring onions and fry gently for about 5 minutes. Mix in the sweetcorn and chilli flakes and set aside.

Put the cornmeal and flour into a mixing bowl with the sugar, salt, baking powder and bicarbonate of soda and mix well. Add the buttermilk, eggs, cooled bacon mixture, melted butter, maple syrup and pepper and mix until well combined.

Put the mixture into the loaf tin and bake for 30-40 minutes until cooked and golden. Remove from the tin, slice and serve warm.

Rosemary bread

MAKES

1 loaf

PREP AND COOK TIME

1 hour 30 minutes

INGREDIENTS

2 eggs, beaten

warm water

1 tsp yeast

400 g | 14 oz | 4 cups strong white bread flour

45 g | 1 ½ oz chopped fresh rosemary

1 tbsp caster (superfine) sugar

60 ml | 2 fl. oz extra virgin olive oil

Grease a loaf tin with butter. Put the eggs in a measuring jug. Add warm water, to make up to the volume of 275 ml. Pour the liquid into a bowl, sprinkle over the yeast, add the flour, rosemary, sugar and olive oil.

Mould the mixture together with your hands, then knead it on a lightly floured surface for 10 minutes until smooth and elastic. Shape into a rectangle and put it into the loaf tin. Loosely cover with cling film and leave in a warm place for 40 minutes, until doubled in size.

Heat the oven to 200°C (180° fan) 400F, gas 6. Bake the bread for 45-50 minutes until golden. Remove the loaf from the tin and place on a wire rack to cool.

Banana and macadamia rolls

MAKES

8 rolls

PREP AND COOK TIME

1 hour

INGREDIENTS

15 g | ½ oz fresh yeast

60 g | 2 oz | ½ cup sugar

45 ml | 1 ½ fl. oz warm milk

300 g | 11 oz | 3 cups strong white flour

2 bananas

1 lemon, juice

25 g | 1 oz | butter, melted

25 g | 1 oz | sugar

50 g | 2 oz | ½ cup macadamia nuts

Crumble the yeast into a small bowl and stir in the sugar and milk. Leave it to stand for a few minutes until frothy. Put the flour into a mixing bowl and pour in the yeast milk. Cover the bowl and leave to stand for 15 minutes.

Mash the bananas with the lemon juice. Add them to the yeast mixture and mix to a smooth dough that leaves the sides of the bowl clean. Cover with a tea towel or cling film and leave to rise in a warm place for 45 minutes.

Heat the oven to 180°C (160° fan) 350F, gas 4. Grease a round, ovenproof dish. Turn out the dough on a floured surface and knead until smooth. Divide into 8 pieces and shape each piece into a ball. Arrange the dough balls in a circle in the baking dish. Cover as before and leave to rise in a warm place for 15 minutes.

Spoon the melted butter over the dough balls and sprinkle with sugar and nuts. Bake for 40 minutes until golden and risen. Remove from the oven and allow the rolls to cool in the dish.

Index